WORKING
AND SURVIVING
IN ORGANISATIONS

WORKING AND SURVIVING IN ORGANISATIONS

A Trainer's Guide to Developing Organisational Skills

Sheila Dainow

JOHN WILEY & SONS

Chichester · New York · Weinheim · Brisbane · Singapore · Toronto

Published 1998 by John Wiley & Sons Ltd,
                   Baffins Lane, Chichester
                   West Sussex PO19 1UD, England

                   National 01243 779777
                   International (+44) 1243 779777
                   e-mail (for orders and customer service enquiries): cs-books@wiley.co.uk
                   Visit our Home Page on http://www.wiley.co.uk
                          or http://www.wiley.com

Other Wiley Editorial Offices

John Wiley & Sons, Inc., 605 Third Avenue,
New York, NY 10158-0012, USA

WILEY-VCH Verlag GmbH, Pappelallee 3,
D-69469 Weinheim, Germany

Jacaranda Wiley Ltd, 33 Park Road, Milton,
Queensland 4064, Australia

John Wiley & Sons (Asia) Pte Ltd, Clementi Loop #02-01,
Jin Xing Distripark, Singapore 129809

John Wiley & Sons (Canada) Ltd, 22 Worcester Road,
Rexdale, Ontario M9W 1L1, Canada

Library of Congress Cataloging-in-Publication Data

Dainow, Sheila, 1937–
    Working and surviving organisations: a trainer's guide to developing
    organisational skills / Sheila Dainow.
        p.   cm.
    Includes bibliographical references and index.
    ISBN 0-471-98151-6 (paper)
    1. Employees—Training of.   2. Organizational effectiveness.
3. Job stress—Prevention.   I. Title.
HF5549.5.T7D338   1998
658.3' 124—dc21   97-44534
                                                       CIP

British Library Cataloguing in Publication Data

A catalogue record for this book is available from the British Library

ISBN 0 471-98151-6

Typeset in 10/12pt Palatino from the author's disks by Mackreth Media Services,
Hemel Hempstead.
Printed and bound in Great Britain by Bookcraft (Bath) Ltd, Midsomer Norton, Somerset.
This book is printed on acid-free paper responsibly manufactured from sustainable forestry,
in which at least two trees are planted for each one used for paper production.

CONTENTS

ABOUT THE AUTHOR

For all her working life, Sheila Dainow has worked with people. Since the 1960s when she worked as a community worker, she trained as a counsellor, tutor, supervisor and therapeutic massage practitioner. She has worked as a trainer for the National Association of Citizens Advice Bureaux and, through her agency Skills With People has taken training into many organisations in the public and private sector. She tutored the Advanced Diplomas in Counselling and Interpersonal Skills at South West London College and the Institute of Education. She is the author of several self-help psychology books and co-editor of the British Association for Counselling's Reader *Counselling*, 1996. In 1997 she became a Fellow of the British Association for Counselling.

PREFACE

Organisations affect us all. Most of the products and services we need to maintain our everyday lives are produced by organisations, and most people who work for a living do so in an organisation. The success of our society depends to a great extent on our ability to create and maintain organised activity. It seems almost too obvious to say that our ability to work effectively together is the key to meeting many of our personal and organisational goals. At best, our job provides us with the money we need to live and purposeful activity which allows us to feel fulfilled and useful. Yet, if you listen to almost any group of people talking about work you will soon realise that, for some, it is enjoyable and rewarding, but, for others, it is little less than torture to be endured. There may be many explanations for this negative state of affairs. Some people may be in an organisation that is too small to allow them to develop their full potential; others find that their organisation is too large and they do not feel personally appreciated. Technological advances and changing economic and social factors mean that change and uncertainty have become an inevitable part of the work scene, and for many people this triggers physical and psychological stress.

This book is intended as a support for those who are responsible for the performance and well-being of staff: managers, human resource officers, trainers and so on. These are the people who are often first aware of the signs of increasing stress among those for whom they are responsible.

Well-planned and presented staff development training initiatives can provide a great deal of practical help, and many organisations use training as a way of helping staff to diminish the effects of stress, thereby ensuring that the organisational objectives are met effectively.

This book offers training structures which will help people understand how they can work in an organisation as happily, as resourcefully and as healthily as possible.

The book is organised so that in each part you will find training objectives to meet issues and problems which seem to arise most often in organisations.

After the scene-setting first chapter, the focus Part I is the organisation itself. The training objectives are to help people understand what makes an organisation tick and why problems can occur for the individuals working in them. In Part II, the spotlight is on issues involved in working with other people. Team development, roles and responsibilities, conflicts and clashes are some of the elements which are explored. Part III provides practical ideas about staying healthy. Here the trainer can introduce and teach simple self-care options to reduce the physical effects of stress. Finally, Part IV considers career development, offering training structures designed to help people move on in their organisation or their career or to manage redundancy or retirement.

The content of the book is drawn from my own experience as a trainer in a variety of organisations as well the increasingly rich collection of theory and practice developed by many practitioners in the field. Source references are provided where possible, although for many of the practical exercises these are lost in the mists of time. Trainers are notoriously squirrel-like in their collection of ideas and material from each other, and so I would like to offer a general acknowledgement to all those colleagues who have been generous in sharing their expertise and from whom I have been privileged to learn so much.

1

SETTING THE SCENE

Designing training for organisations can be a complex affair. Issues which need to be taken into account include the structure of the organisation, training which has already been provided, the nature of the problems which the organisation is trying to solve, the status of training in the organisation and so on. This book is concerned with training specifically designed to help people understand and work effectively within their organisations. Training of this type can make it easier for people to clarify roles, face conflict constructively, manage change and explore their relationships with colleagues, managers and others with whom they work. This chapter aims to set the scene by considering training needs and design.

TRAINING NEEDS AND DESIGN

Running an organisation is like undertaking a journey. You might know exactly where you want to go but if you constantly find yourself ending up somewhere else, you could be said to have a problem! At such times you might stop travelling and analyse the situation.

When an organisation or an individual experiences some problem with the effective and satisfactory achievement of goals, staff training is a possible solution. Training needs analysis, the process of diagnosing the nature of the problem and deciding whether training will actually help, is usually the first step. This is important because not every problem is amenable to resolution by training. If, for instance, the problem is being caused or exacerbated by the way the organisation is structured, no amount of training will, in itself, effect change. The solution is more likely to lie in management decisions regarding possible changes to the system. Returning to the journey analogy, if you discovered that you were constantly misreading the map, you might decide to go on a map-reading course. On the other hand, if you were trying to reach a destination abroad on foot you would have to change your mode of travel for some of the time. As far as I know there is no training course for walking on water—yet!

Training is most likely to be of help when the problem can be linked to issues such as

- a lack of understanding of the processes influencing the situation
- a gap between the skills needed and skills actually demonstrated by post-holders
- lack of relevant knowledge pertaining to the situation
- attitudes which make it difficult to achieve organisational policy
- resistance to change
- high levels of stress causing physical or mental health problems.

Once the problem has been identified as one in which training would be of help, questions, such as, 'Are there any gaps in knowledge or skill which are contributing to the problem?', 'Are there attitudes which need to be explored?', 'What appropriate experience, skills or knowledge do I have to offer?', will help the trainer decide on the most relevant intervention.

The kind of organisational problems which training can probably best address include:

- introduction of new policies or systems
- skills deficits
- conflicts arising between individuals or groups
- implications of new legislation
- lack of team building skills
- increased sickness leave rates due to high stress levels.

The training structures described in this book are modelled on David Kolb's (1984) model of experiential learning. It has been contended by Wimen and Nierhousy (1984) that people generally remember 10% of what they read; 20% of what they hear; 30% of what they see; 50% of what they hear and see; 70% of what they say and write; 80% of what they say as they do something. Kolb's model suggests a systematic approach to ensuring the principle of active participation by learners.

- Stage 1. **Concrete experience:** *'What is happening?'* Personal involvement in experiences.
- Stage 2. **Relative observation:** *'What happened?'* Understanding ideas and situations by reflecting on observation of the experience.
- Stage 3. **Abstract conceptualization:** *'What does it mean?'* Using a logical and systematic approach to problem solving.
- Stage 4. **Active experimentation:** *'What shall I do as a result?'* Practical application in order to achieve goals.

All the training sessions in this book aim to follow this principle of active participation by learners. Wherever possible, lecture inputs are followed by active exercises such as role plays, problem solving, discussions and so on. For experiential learning to be effective, all four stages should be involved. An observation exercise which does not involve the participant in a concrete experience is not sufficient; a role play which is not related to practical application is unlikely to lead to substantial change. Skill training which relies solely on lectures and demonstrations can be amusing, interesting and enlightening, but it will probably remain an intellectual exercise if the participants are not able to practise actively. The exercises usually include some time for reflection and discussion.

WORKING WITH GROUPS

Creating the right atmosphere for participative learning is a skill in itself. It requires the ability to work with large and small groups, to structure activities, manage discussions, present theory inputs, move people on or slow them down when necessary, an understanding of the effect of the psychological dynamic of groups and so on. An organisation is a group; a large organisation will contain many groupings, formal and informal, large and small. Many of the problems which arise in organisations are related in some way or other to how these groups function individually and together. This means bringing an awareness and sensitivity to whatever group dynamic issues may be at play for course participants. Here are some of the concerns which can arise.

Boundaries

Wyn Bramley (1979) identifies five types of boundary which can affect the functioning of a training group. These seem particularly important when the content of the training itself may well revolve around effective boundary management.

1. *Loose or absent boundaries.* Absence or vagueness of boundaries results in confusion about group identity. Sessions not beginning or ending on time; different levels of management attending a course without clarity as to their roles; unclear briefings for group exercises; participants not sure whether they are attending a staff meeting or a training session are all examples of loose or absent boundaries.
2. *Rigid boundaries.* The other side of the coin where the tutor runs the course in an authoritarian style, insisting on absolute attendance, discipline and high standards of work is not satisfactory either. There are some advantages, in that everyone knows where they stand, but a very rigid regime often results in rebellion by those who may feel too strictly controlled.
3. *Boundaries under stress.* Any external threat to the boundaries creates a

reaction. Take for instance a decision by senior management, perhaps for financial reasons, to stop a training course which is proving popular with staff and tutors. Much of the energy of the group will be used in expressing the anxiety and resentment they feel. Safe boundaries are necessary for learning to take place.

4. *Stable boundaries.* Here there are no particular problems; although a certain flatness might be felt as time goes on without the stimulation which danger often brings with it.
5. *Flexible boundaries.* This is probably the most satisfactory situation for which to aim. The boundaries are flexible enough to allow influences from the 'outside' to penetrate, to accept changes in process where necessary, to adapt to changing circumstances without disintegration.

Where the organisational problems which have triggered the need for training are related to bad boundary management, a model of effective boundary management demonstrated by the trainer can be very influential in initiating change.

CONFIDENTIALITY

Group discussion is one obvious way to involve participants actively in their learning. During a discussion, participants can share their views, ask questions for clarification and draw the learning from a group exercise. A discussion which takes place at the beginning of a session can provide useful information as to the group's level of knowledge and experience. Discussion can break up a long lecture or give participants some light relief from a heavy work session.

The issue of confidentiality is an important one. Training which is taking place in an organisation usually means that people who know and work with each other are in the training group. Participants may not feel free to share their thoughts and feelings for obvious reasons. It is useful to address this particular matter at the beginning of any training. People should feel as confident as possible that they will not be gossiped about and be willing to agree not to gossip about others. It is also important for the trainer to be clear and open about his or her contract with the employers so that course participants are aware as to the nature of future contact between the trainer and employers. Is the training, for instance, part of a selection process?

It will help if training exercises, case studies, role plays and so on are designed to address general principles rather than particular situations. For instance, discussion groups can be briefed in various ways to channel the discussion:

- The group is asked to consider differences or similarities; e.g. *'What is the difference between coaching, counselling and supervision?'*.

- The group can be asked to develop lists; e.g. *'What are the necessary components of an ideal reception area?'*
- The group can answer a question; e.g. *'What would you do in these circumstances?'*
- The group can share personal experiences or information; e.g. *'Describe the power structure of your organisation to each other'*.

USING GROUPS TO WIDEN CONTACT

One of the indirect benefits of training is that people are able to widen their range of contacts with others. If the training is taking place in an organisation where people already have some contact with each other, the quality of their relationships can be improved greatly through positive training experiences. People can be given the opportunity to listen to each other and, as a result, understand each other better. They can meet face-to-face with people whom they have only known through the telephone or memos. They can experience themselves as being part of a supportive system rather than as someone struggling to survive in a hostile environment.

FORMAT OF SESSIONS

The following chapters contain as much information as possible to enable your training to be successful. Each chapter focuses on a particular organisational issue and consists of a set of training sessions linked to that particular issue. General training objectives are listed for each session. Sessions consist of *inputs* presented by the trainer and *exercises* for the participants. Sometimes the subject under focus raises issues which might usefully be considered when planning the training. These are placed in the book as they occur, under the heading 'Notes for the Trainer'.

EXERCISE FORMAT

Each session described in the book includes exercises—activities which are designed to help participants clarify their thinking, practise skills or demonstrate theory. The description of each exercise includes:

- the instructions to be given to the group
- timing
- ideal group size
- suggestions as to possible feedback structures
- suggestions for variations where appropriate.

CONCLUDING COMMENTS

Organisations have an immensely important role to play in shaping society today. It must be helpful both for the individuals and for the organisation as a whole if the people who work in the organisation understand them. My hope would be that with the increased insight that training can bring, people would increase their ability to exert some control over their situation. In his foreword of *Organisational Behaviour* (Huczynski and Buchanan, 1991), Professor D.S. Pugh points out that every act of a worker, supervisor, shop steward or managing director rests on interpretations of what has happened, and conjectures about what will happen. He goes on to suggest that attempts to gain understanding which are based only on our own experiences will inevitably be of limited use as we meet new experiences. We need new information and insights to help us to meet the challenges facing us. This book sets out to describe training structures which will enable trainers to provide creative, practical and effective help to people who are trying to overcome some of the problems of working in organisations.

REFERENCES

Kolb, D. (1984). *Experiential Learning*. Prentice Hall.
Wiman, B. & Nierhousy, J. (1991). *Experiential Learning*. Prentice Hall.
Bramley, W. (1979). *Group Tutoring: Concepts and Case Studies*. Kogan Page.
Huczynski, A. & Buchanan, D. (1991). *Organizational Behaviour*. Prentice Hall International (UK) Ltd.

I

UNDERSTANDING ORGANISATIONS

2

THE CULTURE OF THE ORGANISATION

Many people who experience their work as stressful are struggling to deal with the destructive physical and emotional effects of too much pressure. What often makes the situation worse for them is that they may not really understand the root causes of the stress they feel. There are many aspects of working life which can create stress, some of which may well be to do with the nature and culture of the organisation. To a great extent this is outside the control of any individual to change. However, most practitioners in the field of stress reduction teach that the first step towards managing stress is to gain a better understanding of the way stress actually develops.

Part I contains training designed to help people understand something about the nature of organisations. Although organisations are made up of individuals, each with his or her particular talents, skills and expectations, once these people are in an organisation they are inevitably influenced by the organisation itself.

If you travel to another country you will become aware of the differences in the way things are organised; if you stay for any length of time you will notice the different traditions, beliefs, habits of behaviour and values. You may become aware of the way this particular country is affected by its history. These are the clues which tell you about the culture of this place.

In much the same way, each organisation creates a culture which affects the people in it. In some cases problems arise because key personnel are in some way at odds with the culture of the organisation. New people may find the culture very different from the one they have just left. Sometimes the prevailing culture, acceptable to the workers in the organisation, does not match changes in society and stands in the ways of objectives being met.

Training can bring about greater understanding as to how some difficulties might be by-products of the structure or culture of the organisation itself. This can, in turn, clarify how individuals may need to adapt their own behaviour or make changes in the organisation.

This kind of training would be particularly useful for management trainees or for staff of organisations where change is taking place.

SESSION 1: FOUR CULTURES

Training objectives

1. To clarify a working definition of organisation.
2. To explore four types of organisation cultures as defined by Charles Handy (1976).
3. To identify strengths and weaknesses of each and to consider the implications of these.
4. To enable comparison with the participants' own organisations.

Notes for the Trainer

Because culture is largely a matter of perception, it is difficult to define precisely. You know it is there because you experience it but it is often hard to convert feelings into concrete evidence. Training sessions like the one which follows helps to increase understanding of processes which may be unconsciously influencing people's behaviour. The session begins with an exercise.

The session includes some theory input which could be provided as a printed hand-out or given as a brief lecture.

Exercise 2.1: What is an Organisation?

Group Structure: Brainstorm followed by work in pairs.
Timing: 10–15 minutes.
Materials: Flip chart and pen for trainer

Process: Explain to the group that this session is concerned with understanding organisations and ask people to call out any organisations to which they belong or have belonged in the past. List these on a flip chart. When the group run out of suggestions, ask them to identify the elements present in the groups they have identified which lead them to think of them as *Organisations*. Write up this second list which might look like this:

- Involves people
- Structured activity
- Agreed aims and objectives

- Identified boundaries
- Administrative structures
- An understood hierarchy of power
- Knowing who is 'in' and who is 'out'
- Shared values, etc.

When the two lists are developed as far as possible, ask people to work in pairs for 10 minutes to come up with a definition for the word 'Organisation'.

Discuss these definitions with the group as a whole.

A example of a definition: *Organisations are social arrangements for the controlled performance of collective goals* (Huczynski & Buchanan, 1991).

Having established a shared working definition for organisations, you can move on to focus on the concept of *Culture*.

Exercise 2.2: Comparing Cultures

Group Structure: Short input followed by group discussion.
Timing: 15–10 minutes.

Process: Explain that your aim is to identify factors which affect the culture of an organisation and to raise awareness as to how each organisation creates its own particular culture.

Start with a brief input, listing the factors which influence the culture of an organisation, for example:

- Size
- Personality of creators
- Age of organisation
- History
- Achievements/failures
- Aims
- Place
- People employed, and so on.

Variation: Ask the group to brainstorm a list of factors. When the list is complete, ask participants to think of two different organisations with which they have been or are now associated.

> Working in pairs or small groups, ask the participants to compare the cultures of the organisations they have identified. Group discussion can focus on the effect of each factor.

Having focused on the meaning of organisation and culture, you can move on to describing different types of culture.

Trainer Input

Charles Handy suggests that organisational culture can be divided into four types: Power, Role, Task and Person.

The POWER culture is most likely to be found in small organisations which have been started by an entrepreneur or a person with a very clear vision and philosophy. It could be drawn as a web or a wheel, as shown in Figure 2.1.

This is a culture which depends on a central figure providing the driving force of the organisation. From this central figure, channels of communication spread out to other individuals or groups. All the communication moves through the central figure. The organisation works on anticipating the wishes and following instructions from the central power source. Because control is exercised so clearly, there tends to be little bureaucracy.

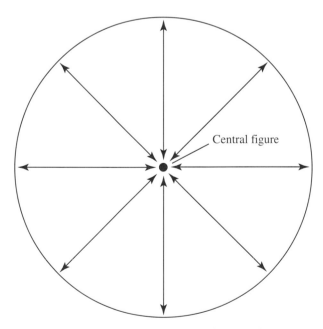

Figure 2.1: Power culture 'The Wheel'

Successful organisations with this culture have the ability to move quickly and can react well to threat or danger.

Companies that start as family businesses often take on this culture. The structure works well at the beginning but can run into problems if it does not adapt to changing circumstances. For instance, if the central figure dies or retires, the company may decline. If it grows too large, it can only succeed by spawning other satellite organisations. A web will break if it is spread too far and organisations with this culture cannot easily deal with increasing size.

The ROLE culture is probably the most bureaucratic. It is exemplified by logic and, if drawn, would look most like a Greek temple (see Figure 2.2).

This organisation invests its strength in functions or specialities—the columns. Each column represents a department or section which is strong in its own right. Procedures control the interaction between the pillars; for instance, there are clearly defined rules as to how communication takes place, how decisions are made and how disputes are resolved.

In this culture a person's job is more important than his or her personality. Success depends on each person fulfilling his or her role—doing no more and no less. The organisation is co-ordinated at the top by a narrow band of senior management and it is generally only necessary for departments to communicate with each other through this band.

The TASK culture is job or project led. It could be drawn as a net, as in Figure 2.3. Some strands of the net are stronger than others and much of the power and influence lies at the points at which the strands of the net meet—the 'knots'. The entire energy of this culture is directed towards getting the job done. The culture aims to bring together all the resources which would be best for the success of the job.

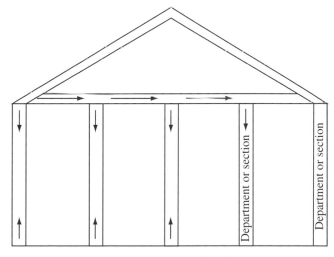

Figure 2.2: Role culture 'The Temple'

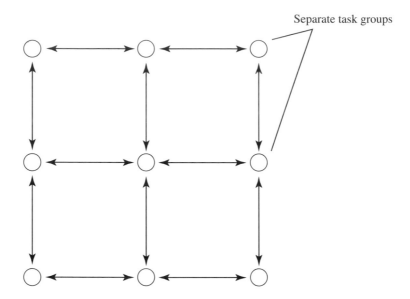

Figure 2.3: Task culture 'The Net'

Power is invested more in expertise than in personal power. Control might be retained by top management who may be responsible for allocating projects and resources, but the day-to-day working is in the control of the group concerned.

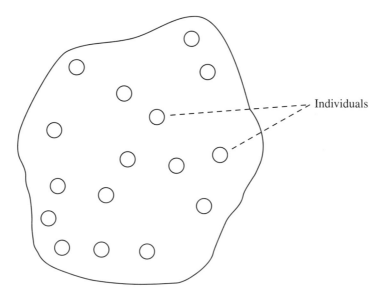

Figure 2.4: Person culture 'The Cluster'

In our last example, the PERSON culture, the individual is the central point. Whatever structure does exist is there to serve and assist the individuals within it. It could be drawn as a cluster, as in Figure 2.4.

This culture is most likely to be present when a particular group decides it is in their best interest to get together in order to fulfil their own objectives and share space and resources. They aim to do this with the minimum of imposed structures. Partnerships of professionals like barristers, dentists, counsellors are all examples of the person culture. Control can only be exerted by mutual consent; individuals can leave the organisation but it is difficult for the organisation to eject the individual.

Exercise 2.3: Assets and Liabilities

Group Structure: If the group is large enough, split it into four small groups. Otherwise, work in pairs or threes.
Timing: 30 minutes.
Materials: Large sheet of paper and pens for each group to list points.

Process: Allocate one of the cultures to each small group and ask them to discuss what they see to be the assets and liabilities of the culture they have been given. Each group then presents their ideas and a general discussion can follow.

The lists of assets and liabilities of each culture could include the following points:

Assets	*Liabilities*
Power culture	
Such a culture can create a strong and proud atmosphere.	Dependent on the person in the centre.
Ability to move quickly.	Cannot grow too large.
Can react decisively to threat.	Individuals can suffer from low morale due to competitive atmosphere or lack of personal power.
Role culture	
Very successful in a stable environment.	This culture makes it difficult to manage change.
Individuals know their place and role in the organisation.	Slow to perceive the need for change.

Organisation offers security and predictability.

Individuals can often become specialists in their particular field.

Structure can be frustrating for the individual who wants more control.

Task culture

Very adaptable as groups can be reformed to meet changing needs.

Speed in reacting to change.

Individuals have high control over their work.

Many theories of management and organisations encourage this kind of culture.

Works well when making the product or providing the service is the most important thing

Hard to produce economies of scale.

There may be less depth of expertise or specialisation

Overall control is difficult.

Morale can decline if resources are limited.

Person culture

Provides a high level of power and responsibility to individuals.

Gives a great deal of 'job satisfaction'.

Decision making very slow as consensus is needed.

Not many organisations can operate entirely within this culture because overall management of objectives is difficult.

Notes for the Trainer

This kind of exercise raises awareness to the possibility—and even necessity—of flexibility in organisation design. One culture may be ideal for a particular set of circumstances like starting off an organisation. However, when the circumstances change, another culture may be more appropriate.

Certain types of people will be happy, effective workers in one kind of culture and not in another. People who blossom in a person culture may wither in role culture. Some people prefer the tighter role prescriptions and high levels of predictability in the role culture.

Because individual skill and talent are influential in power and task cultures, greater care needs to be paid to the selection and appraisal of staff in them.

You may find that there are people in your training group who are unhappy in the organisation and who can trace at least some of that unhappiness to the fact that they are in a culture which conflicts with their own personal needs. This kind of training session at least allows them space to consider the implications of this and to decide whether to modify their own needs in or move to a more congenial work setting.

This next exercise takes the work of this session further by encouraging participants to match their own values and beliefs with that of their organisation.

Exercise 2.4: You and Your Organisation

Group structure: Individual work followed by group discussion
Timing: 30 minutes.
Materials: Quiz form for each person.

Process: Give out quiz and check that everyone understands what is required.

YOU AND YOUR ORGANISATION QUIZ

There is space to rate each of the following statements from 1 (that which represents the dominant view of you or your organisation) to 4 (that which represents it least). Do the rating exercise twice—once for your organisation and once for yourself.

The statements are related to the four types of culture and the point of the exercise is to identify the prevailing culture of your organisation and compare it to your own preference.

Organ-
zisation Self

1 *The first priority of a good employer should be:*
. . . .   to be in control of all aspects of the organisation.
. . . .   to ensure that people adhere to organisational procedures.
. . . .   that the job gets done.
. . . .   to provide a working environment which is sensitive to the needs of individuals.

2 *The first priority of a good employee should be:*
. . . .   to put the interest of the boss first.
. . . .   conscientiously follow the laid-down procedures of the organisation.
. . . .   to the successful completion of the task at hand.
. . . .   self-development.

3 *In order to do well in the organisation you should:*

....   have a strong drive for power and be competitive.

....   be conscientious and responsible and, above all, loyal to the organisation.

....   have technical expertise and, above all, want to get the job done.

....   able to develop very good personal relationships and have a commitment to personal growth and development.

4 *The individual is treated by the organisation as if he or she was:*

....   at the complete disposal of those with a higher position.

....   bound by the organisational contracts and systems.

....   equal to everyone else working to meet common goals.

....   as worth while and interesting in his or her own right.

5   *People are best motivated by:*

....   power and authority; reward and punishment.

....   clear procedures and contracts; knowing where they stand.

....   achieving goals.

....   caring for others and being cared for by others in the organisation.

6 *It is acceptable for one person to control another if:*

....   the organisation has vested power and authority in this person.

....   it is prescribed by the role this person plays in the organisation.

....   if he or she, by virtue of deeper knowledge or skill, is more able to complete the task at hand.

....   if the person being controlled accepts that the control will lead to greater growth and development.

7 *People work because:*

....   they believe in the person at the top, hope for a reward and/or are afraid of the consequences of under-achieving.

....   they value the system and believe in keeping to contracts.

....   of the satisfaction of successfully completing a task.

....   they enjoy it and value contact with other people.

8 *People work best in a team when:*
.... required to by a higher authority.
.... required to by the formal system.
.... teamwork would lead to the completion of the task more quickly or successfully.
.... they find the other members of the team likeable, stimulating and helpful.

9 *Conflicts are best resolved by:*
.... decisive intervention from the top.
.... reference to the rules and procedures laid down by the organisation.
.... focusing discussion on how the task is being affected by the conflict and seeking solutions which would lead to the completion of the task.
.... full and deep discussion of the personal issues involved.

10 *Decisions should be made by:*
.... the person with most power and authority.
.... the person whose job description covers that particular area of authority.
.... the person with most knowledge or expertise about that particular area.
.... the people most involved and affected by the outcome.

Adapted from a quiz designed by Dr Roger Harrison and contained in Charles Handy's *Understanding Organisations* (1976).

When the participants have finished marking the quiz, ask them to add up the scores for the all the first statements, and then the second, third and fourth statements (i.e. a score of 10 for the first statement would mean that it scored top in all questions).

There are several interesting angles to this exercise which could be picked up in the discussion: for example, the implications of the perceived dominant culture of the organisation; the implications of any differences between the culture of the organisation and personal preference.

Notes for the Trainer

This session works well as an introduction to the concept of organisational culture for trainee managers, or an awareness-raising exercise for recruitment and selection training. It can provide a foundation for a training designed to help a group analyse problems it is facing. As the trainer you will need to have worked out how you will link this to whatever comes next in your training event.

Our next chapter continues the focus on understanding organisations by exploring some psychological dynamics which affect the work of an organisation and the individuals in it.

REFERENCES

Handy, C.B. (1976). *Understanding Organisations*. Penguin.
Huczynski, A. & Buchanan, D. (1991). *Organizational Behaviour*. Prentice Hall.

3

PSYCHOLOGY AND ORGANISATIONS

This chapter highlights the importance of understanding the way that individual unconscious drives can affect an organisation as a whole. There are obvious links with the previous chapter in which we explored the way that an organisation can develop a particular culture which then affects each individual. Many work organisations are aware of the importance of understanding the psychology of personality. One result of this is that the use of psychological testing in the recruitment process seems to be increasing.

Organisations obviously want to hire people who will be good at their job and often use personality tests to try to uncover a picture of what the applicant is *really* like. This is most often done by using some kind of questionnaire which is designed to reveal deep-lying aspects of the personality.

Understanding a little about why people behave the way they do is not only useful for the recruitment process, but can also have a profound effect on the way individuals relate to each other and the job in hand. The inclusion of this kind of training in a staff development programme can raise awareness as to how people's behaviour might be influenced by their own unconscious drives. With this knowledge, people are more able to control their responses to situations which might cause them problems.

SESSION 2: HOW PERSONAL NEEDS AFFECT AN ORGANISATION

Training Objectives

1. To demonstrate the importance of meeting personal needs.
2. To introduce Maslow's theory of the hierarchy of needs.
3. To consider the implications of unmet needs to an organisation.

Trainer Input

From our earliest childhood we learn to attach meaning to the things and people around us. We transfer experience from one similar situation to another; we listen to the instructions which our parents and other adults give us about ourselves and life in general; we watch how they manage and decide whether or not to copy them. We develop a script for our life. Eric Berne (1974), the originator of Transactional Analysis, wrote: 'The destiny of every human being is decided by what goes on inside his skull when he is confronted with what goes on outside his skull.'

We seek to survive by creating a secure and meaningful life for ourselves. This sense of security depends to a large extent on our ability to predict the outcomes of our own behaviour and that of others. The meaning in our life is dependent on how well the way we perceive the world fits in with what actually happens to us. Each one of us is motivated by a set of needs which must be fulfilled in order for us to develop and grow.

Abraham Maslow (1970) identified seven innate needs:

1. *Physiological needs basic to human survival:* e.g. light, food, water, sex.
2. *Safety needs:* e.g. shelter, security, order, predictability, freedom from threat.
3. *Affiliation needs:* e.g. social relationships, affection, love, a feeling of belonging.
4. *Esteem needs:* e.g. respect, achievement, confidence, recognition, attention, importance.
5. *Self-realisation needs:* to allow development of our fullest potential.
6. *Freedom of expression needs,* leading to an influence on social conditions, freedom of speech and the encouragement of a fair society.
7. *Cognitive needs:* to know and understand; to tackle the unknown; to 'make sense' of our world and our life.
8. *Spiritual needs:* to develop a sense of something greater than ourselves.

He drew them as a pyramid with the most basic needs at the bottom (Figure 3.1). His basic premise was that we unconsciously organise our behaviour to meet the categories of need in an order of urgency, with those at the bottom taking precedence over those further up.

The first two sets of needs, physiological and safety, are essential to our survival and if they are not met, we die. Affiliation and esteem needs are about the quality of the contact we have as a result of our relationships with others. If these needs are not met, we can feel inferior, helpless, discouraged, depressed—that 'life is not worth living'. Maslow felt that self-actualisation needs are the human ultimate goal. He also argues that the last two needs on

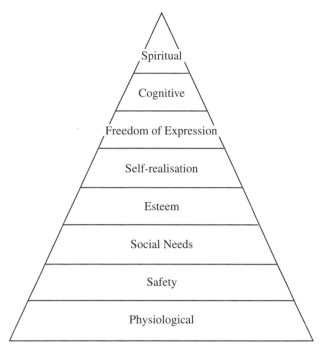

Figure 3.1: Maslow's Pyramid

the list—i.e. the need for freedom of enquiry and to know and understand—
were not so much at the top of a pyramid but actually necessary for the other
five needs to be satisfactorily met.

Maslow suggested the following 'rules' relating to the pyramid:

1. A need is not an effective motivator unless the one beneath it has been more
   or less met. For example, you are not likely to worry too much about the
   colour of the carpet if you are in danger of losing your house altogether.
2. When one need is met, your preoccupation will be with the next highest,
   unless or until the first need becomes unsatisfied. As you become hungrier,
   your attention will move to your hunger. When you have eaten you can
   concentrate again on whatever you were doing—unless you become
   hungry again.
3. Constant, continued dissatisfaction of these needs affects mental health.
4. We have an innate desire to work our way up the hierarchy.
5. The self-actualisation need cannot be satisfied in the same way as those
   below it. If we do actually experience fulfilling our potential, we will want
   to do more of it.

Exercise 3.1: Pyramids of Need

Group Structure: Pairs or small groups
Timing: 20–30 minutes
Materials: Large sheets of paper for each group. Papers can be prepared in advance with the pyramid of needs already drawn:

Process: Ask participants whether they can recognise the needs in Maslow's theory in their own behaviour, identifying things they do to satisfy each of the needs.

Ask each group to fill in each section with some of the behaviour they identified earlier. These sheets can then be displayed and discussed.

This exercise is to encourage people to compare the theory with their personal experience. The next exercise aims to use Maslow's theory to understand its implications for an organisation.

Exercise 3.2: The Pyramid and the Organisation

Group Structure: Individual work
Timing: 15–20 minutes
Materials: Similar worksheet to previous exercise

Process: Using a fresh outline of the pyramid, divided into the five sections, ask participants to fill in how they feel each need could be addressed by an organisation. For example:

SELF-ACTUALISATION
Challenging tasks
Promotion
Creativity
Self direction over work activities

ESTEEM
Positive feedback
'Official' recognition
Prestigious job title

AFFILIATION
Sports/social clubs
Office outings/parties
Time for informal activities
Relaxation area

SAFETY
Health insurance
Good pension provision
Attention to health and safety
'No redundancy' guarantee

PHYSIOLOGICAL
Free/subsidised canteen or
allowance for lunches
Reasonable wages
Subsidised housing
Comfortable working conditions

The next stage of the exercise is to ask participants to identify how their organisation meets these needs at the present time. This can lead to a discussion of the implication of unmet needs. This, in turn, can give pointers as to how some organisational problems may be caused or enhanced by the conscious or unconscious reaction of people to the unmet needs.

You might choose to end this exercise with a goal-setting exercise encouraging people to decide how they might begin to fill some of the gaps they identified.

SESSION 3: THE UNCONSCIOUS AT WORK

Training Objectives

1. To describe psychological defence mechanisms.
2. To show how personal defence mechanisms can affect the organisation.

Notes for the Trainer

This particular session is focused on the unconscious defence mechanisms as described by Sigmund Freud (1953–1974) as an explanation of a great deal of human behaviour. People are sometimes resistant to (a) Sigmund Freud and/or (b) accepting that some apparently rational behaviour stems from the unconscious as a defence of our self-image or ego so you may need to give thought as to how you introduce this session.

However most people do experience the kind of behaviour which arises from the various defences both within themselves and from others. Labelling these behaviours provides a way of ordering them in order to consider possible modification where the behaviour is causing a problem.

Exercise 3.3: What Did You Do?

Group Structure: Individual work.
Timing: 5 minutes.

Process: Ask participants to think of a recent time when they were under stress. Tell them that they will be discussing this with a small group so they should not select a situation which they do not want to share with others. In fact, they do not have to choose something very significant—a small event will be just as acceptable (e.g. someone else taking a parking space you have just lined up; buying something which turned out to be a mistake).

Ask them to jot down what they remember thinking, feeling and doing at the time. Encourage them to keep the three elements separate.

Suggest that participants keep these notes available while you present the input.

Trainer Input

There is growing awareness of the effect of stress on the ability of people to work effectively and happily. In this session we are going to explore the issue using the theory that some of our behaviour arises from unconscious drives.

A well-known case study presented by psychoanalyst Isabel Menzies (1960) demonstrated that high levels of anxiety and stress among nurses in a London teaching hospital was, to some extent, due to the way the hospital defined the nurses' role as well as the inherent stresses in the job itself.

In the study, the organisation was itself treated as though it was the 'patient'. The presenting problem was that the hospital was finding it difficult to complete the training of as many student nurses as it needed. The nurses had a very high rate of sickness and many dropped out of the training altogether.

Through a process of interviews and observation, it became clear that the nurses were suffering from a great deal of anxiety and tension about their role in the hospital. Perhaps because the consultant was a psychoanalyst, she was interested in exploring the source of the anxiety. She found that it lay in the job itself. These young people were being asked to do a job which had some very unpleasant and frightening aspects. The nursing of very sick or injured people involves dealing with blood, vomit, excrement and so on. Sometimes, in spite of everything the carers can do, the patient dies.

The student nurses were inevitably experiencing deep emotions—the intensity of which were sometimes frightening and disturbing in themselves. As well as dealing with their reactions to the work with patients, the students were also affected by the strong emotions of the patients and relatives. Patients were not always grateful for the care—sometimes they were angry and resentful; sometimes they discounted the students because of their youth. Relatives, in dealing with their own grief, would complain about or blame the nurses. Clearly, the young students were in a highly volatile emotional atmosphere.

The way the hospital dealt with this problem was to create a system in which the nurse was largely protected from feeling anything. Each job was rigidly defined and the nurse was expected to carry the tasks out almost like a machine. A machine does not have to think or feel or question.

By falling into this way of working, nurses were relieved of any sense of responsibility for what happened to the patients. Student nurses were also moved from ward to ward so that they could not form any lasting attachment to individual patients.

In this way the powerful emotions were denied, but did not disappear. What seems to happen in this kind of situation is that the denied feelings lodge in the unconscious. So, by not allowing the nurses even to admit that they had the feelings, the hospital greatly increased their emotional turmoil. This turbulence was seen to be the root of the anxiety felt by the nurses. For some of them the level of anxiety became too great to bear and so they dropped out of training or fell ill.

Exercise 3.4: Feelings

Group Structure: Individual work and pairs
Timing: 10 minutes

Process: Ask the group members to consider whether there are any aspects of their work about which they have strong emotional feelings. Suggest that they then work in pairs to consider how the organisation helps or hinders them in managing their response.

This could lead to further work in designing a system which would allow for the acceptance and expression of these feelings.

Trainer Input

It is not difficult to understand the problem that organisations sometimes have in dealing with strong emotions. After all, organisations are made up of individuals and, as we saw with Maslow, each of us has a need to feel comfortable, safe and secure. This is such a basic need that we develop ways of defending our inner selves (our ego) against disturbing or distressing emotions.

Sigmund Freud first described these strategies as defence mechanisms. The behaviours which he described seem to ring true for many people and the labels have entered our everyday language.

Projection

Sometimes, if we feel very uncomfortable with certain thoughts or feelings we assign them to someone else. It is as if we project them from within ourselves to an external source. This process is easy to notice with powerful impulses like sex and aggression. Some people do seem to be overly concerned with the detail of the sexual or violent behaviour of others. It may be that their righteousness stems from their defence against emotions within themselves which they would find frightening or unable to contain.

Projection can also be at the root of our strong reaction to a particular person. Once again, if there is some element of our own personality with which we feel uncomfortable, it may become easier to face when we see it on someone else.

Exercise 3.5: Projection.

Group Structure: Whole group.
Timing: 20 minutes.

Process: This exercise involves visualisation, so you need to ask participants to relax and concentrate on their breathing for a moment or two. Explain that you are going to suggest something for them to imagine and encourage them to stay aware of their thoughts and feelings as the exercise progresses. Ask them to think of a person they don't like very much. Give them time to build up the picture of the person in their mind, seeing them doing whatever it is that causes the problem. Then ask them to imagine themselves as this person, speaking, moving, acting in the way the person does. Once again, give them time to build up the picture in their mind's eye. Then ask them to return in their mind to being themselves and imagine that the other person is with them. Remind them to notice how they think and feel and then allow them to open their eyes.

Suggest they jot down the answers to these questions:

- What exactly is it about the other person that I don't like?
- How easily could I imagine myself doing those things?
- Is it at all possible that I could act in this way if I allowed myself?

A general discussion can follow.

Variation: You can repeat the exercise, this time asking people to imagine someone they like and admire. It is a good way of balancing the exercise and people can become aware of positive potential in themselves which they may be denying.

Notes for the Trainer

These kind of sessions can be very effective in giving people a different perspective of interpersonal conflicts. Introducing an interesting general theory about human behaviour can feel less threatening than sessions which are specifically directed towards sorting out personal disagreements and differences. It is usually possible to gently direct the discussion towards relating the theory to people's personal experience.

The other defence mechanisms which can be applied to this study are:

Sublimation
This is the process by which we repress an impulse or feeling which feels too dangerous to express directly in its pure form. Art, poetry, etc., might be examples of how this energy is converted into a creative and positive force. Many forms of competition can be seen as efforts to sublimate unacceptable aggressive instincts—no one actually kills anyone in order to win a game of tennis or football, for instance, although the games can be played at great levels of intensity.

Displacement

This is similar to sublimation in that the original impulse is not expressed directly. Here, the emotion doesn't change form but is displaced onto something or someone else. This is one way of understanding the process of scapegoating. If something bad is happening to you, it can be tempting to put the blame on someone else. The feelings can then be vented on this person.

Rationalisation

This is the way we prove our 'rightness' or 'goodness' in situations in which we would otherwise feel 'wrong' or 'bad'. Take, for example, failing to succeed at an interview. We could tell ourselves that we didn't want the job anyway; that the interviewers didn't know what they were doing; that it would be better for us to stay where we were in an attempt to feel better about our failure or rejection.

   Rationalisation also comes into play when we are doing something which we know is wrong. Someone who, for instance, breaks the speed limit might tell themselves that everyone does it; that the speed limit itself causes frustration and therefore accidents and so on.

Reaction Formation

One of the ways we deal with the fear of being overwhelmed by the depth of our feeling towards something is by denouncing it vehemently in other people and taking on the opposite belief for ourselves.

   A woman manager who is uncertain about her decision to put her career development first might, for instance, deal with her anxiety by expressing scorn or contempt towards women who stay at home looking after a family.

Exercise 3.6: Acting Defence Mechanisms.

Group Structure: Small groups.
Timing: 30 minutes plus discussion time.

Process: Having given the above brief input describing defence mechanisms, ask participants to work in small groups and, taking each defence mechanism, make up a brief scene which might take place in a work setting demonstrating that particular defence.

The scenes can then be described or acted out, followed by discussion.

Notes for the Trainer

It is obvious that the focus of this particular training is on personal relationships. Research studies have shown that the quality of social relationships at work can have a therapeutic effect on people who are under pressure or suffering from stress. Henderson and Argyle's (1985) study found that while the support of one's partner is most important when there was a crisis, like the loss of a job, it was colleagues who were more important when there was continuous stress at work.

In training that is intended to help an organisation run more smoothly, it is useful to pay attention to the quality of the relationships between staff. Where there is friction, it is possible that the people involved have only given it superficial thought. This is fine when those involved are able to put their personal feelings aside and concentrate on the job. However, as we have seen, these feelings, whatever their cause, have a way of making themselves felt. It may come as a surprise to some people to realise that they may be reacting, not to the person they believe they know—but to their *perception* of that person. It may be a greater surprise to learn that their perception is influenced by past experiences. An even greater surprise may be the realisation that other people may be reacting in the same way to us!

One of the problems, of course, is that because this process is largely unconscious it is more difficult to understand and control.

Transactional Analysis (TA), the psychotherapy created by Eric Berne, offers a particularly accessible method of analysing social interaction and is often used in management or staff development training. The next section of this chapter uses some of this theory.

SESSION 4: COMMUNICATION PATTERNS

Training Objectives

1. To introduce TA theory of communication.
2. To provide opportunities for applying theory to practice.

Trainer Input

Eric Berne (1964), the creator of Transactional Analysis (TA), believed that our personality consists of a parental, adult or child ego state, and that we can shift with varying degrees of readiness from one to another. An ego state is a set of related thoughts, feelings and actions.

Eric Berne's view was that everyone carries within their personality the potential for thinking, feeling and acting in three quite different ways (Figure 3.2).

1. As our parents or parent figures might have done
2. As the adult we are now
3. As the child we once were.

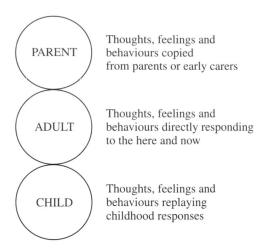

Figure 3.2: The ego states (1)

Simply stated, the Parent Ego State is the part of the personality representing all the instructions and guidance we acquired through intimate association with our parents and other authority figures of our childhood. It is often compared to a vast filing system or database containing all the 'shoulds'; 'oughts'; 'dont's; 'dos' collected from those early days.

The Parent Ego State can be divided into two parts: the Nurturing Parent and the Critical Parent.

Whenever we are thinking, feeling or acting in ways which are a copy of a parent or parent figure, we could be said to be in our Parent Ego State.

The Adult Ego State could be seen as the problem solver. Rational and objective, it provides clear thinking and analysis. Any time we are thinking, feeling and acting in response to what is happening in the present moment, we could be said to be in our Adult state. It is the Adult we call upon when we need to be objective, to separate facts from opinion, to analyse and compute the effects of alternatives, and so on.

The Child Ego State is often considered to be the most creative part of a personality. Behaviour activated by the Child is referred to as child-like rather than childish. Childishness tends to denote immaturity, whereas much of the behaviour originating from the Child Ego State is creative, intuitive, spon-taneous and joyful.

The Child Ego State can also be divided into two parts. The Natural or Free Child is distinguished by its spontaneous enjoyment of life, curiosity and need for affection. The Adapted Child results from the changes that we need to make in order to achieve the social behaviour that makes us acceptable in the adult world. Thus, the picture (Figure 3.3) becomes a little more complex.

It is our Adult which, by moderating between the confusion that can result

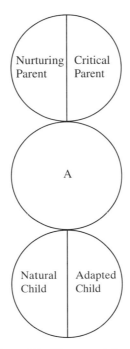

Figure 3.3: The ego states (2)

from acting unconsciously from the Parent or Child Ego State, keeps us attaining objectives in our best interest.

The following are examples of how each ego state might react.

Alison is consider applying for a senior management post:

P   It's not appropriate for women to be in senior posts where they might have to manage men.
A   I am fully qualified for this post; I'd like to accept the challenge.
C   I want the job but men won't like me if I'm in a senior position over them!

David is a manager who is very overloaded; he could delegate to his staff:

P   I'll never be able to trust anyone to do the job as well as you.
A   I can't manage all of this work myself; I have trained my staff and there are tasks they are well able to manage.
C   I'll be in bad trouble if they get it wrong.

Exercise 3.7: Ego States
Group Structure: Individual work followed by discussion.
Timing: 20–30 minutes.

Process: Having described the ego states and given some examples, ask participants to take a problem they have recently faced and write out how each ego state reacted. Which ego state was it that actually dealt with the problem? What might have changed if they had consciously engaged a different ego state?

Trainer Input

Ways to Pinpoint Ego States

We are always giving clues as to which ego state is dominating our behaviour, and you can pinpoint ego states if you know what to look for. There are many clues in posture, facial expression, tone of voice, choice of language, etc. Although you could not be absolutely sure in labelling an ego state, in many cases the origins of remarks or actions are fairly clear.

Exercise 3.8: Picking up the Clues.

Group Structure: Whole group plus discussion.
Timing: 10 minutes.

Process: Provide participants with the following statements and ask them to decide from which ego state each comes:

- 'Don't give up. I know you can do it.' (Nurturing Parent)
- 'Do I have to explain everything?' (Critical Parent)
- 'I shouldn't have to do this—it's too hard for me.' (Adapted Child)
- 'I'm really enjoying this—it's exciting.' (Free Child)
- 'This job will take half-an-hour; then I'll be ready for the meeting.' (Adult)
- 'It's not fair, I've been doing my best but no one seems to co-operate.' (Adapted Child)
- 'You should have finished by now.' (Critical Parent)
- 'I'm very angry.' (Free Child)

Although the answers given are the most likely, you will probably find that participants make other suggestions which seem just as possible. This begins to make it clear that *how* people say something is usually more important than *what* they say.

Here are some of the indicators of ego states which can be given as a hand out:

	Body Language	Speech	Tone
PARENT	Looking down over rim of glasses.	'You should . . . ' 'You ought . . . ' 'You must . . . '	Harsh Judgement Soothing
	Pointing an accusing finger.	'Why don't you?' 'Keep calm' 'You disappoint me'	Indignant Commanding Comforting
	Hands on hips, head thrown back.	'Poor thing'	
ADULT	Straight, relaxed stance.	'The probability is . . . '	Relaxed Assertive
	Active listening.	'What are the facts?'	Deliberative Thoughtful
	Regular eye contact.	'How do you feel about . . . '	Calm Confident
	Attentive.		
CHILD	Forlorn appearance.	'I want . . . ' 'I wish . . . '	Appealing Complaining
	Drooping shoulders.	'Gosh . . . ' 'I should . . . '	Nagging Indignant
	Withdrawal.	'If only . . . '	Cheerful
	Scowling.	'It's not fair'	Protesting
	Sulking.	'One day . . . '	Grumbling
	Skipping.	'Great!'	Sullen
	Hugging.		
	Twinkling eyes.		

Notes for the Trainer

This is a very brief introduction to the TA theory of Ego States. The amount of time you spend on it depends on the level of personal work you are aiming to introduce into the training session. If you want to take it further, books such as Ian Stewart and Vann Joines' *TA Today* (1987) will be of great help.

The purpose in including it here is as a preparation for an understanding as to how communication between people can break down. The next part of the session focuses on the way that Eric Berne analysed communication transactions.

Trainer Input

People communicate with each other on two levels. At the first, 'top', level we exchange information, ask questions, give instructions, explain and so on. At the second, 'underneath', level we are reinforcing our feelings about ourselves and each other. It is at this 'feeling' level that we make 'transactions' with each other when we communicate. Such transactions at work are very important; on the one hand, they allow us to feel secure and free to concentrate on working as productively as possible. If, on the other hand, we end up feeling insecure as a result of the quality of the contact, our energy will be tied up in emotional conflict which inevitably interferes with working.

The nature of the transaction that two people make with each other will result from the particular combination of their respective ego states in action when they communicate. There are three basic kinds of transactions: complementary, crossed and ulterior.

Complementary
A complementary transaction is one in which the initiator gets the kind of response expected. Here are a couple of examples:

MARY: Do you know where my diary is?
JANE: It's on your desk.
(A simple question and answer—Adult to Adult.)

JEFFREY: These trainees think they know it all.
ADRIAN: You're absolutely right—they're all the same.
(These are two Critical Parents confirming each other's (unevaluated) attitudes.)

JONATHON: I'm feeling very low today.
KATHERINE: I'm so sorry; sit down and let me get you a cup of tea.
(Here, Jonathon's child is soothed by Katherine's Nurturing Parent.)

The diagrams of these transactions (Figure 3.4) show how the lines tracing the ego states are parallel.

Complementary transactions can continue indefinitely as long as the lines remain parallel. They often leave people feeling good because the flow of stimulus and response results in needs for attention, stimulus and so on being met.

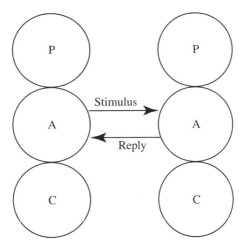

Figure 3.4: A complementary transaction: Adult to Adult

Exercise 3.9: Complementary Transactions

Group Structure: Individual work followed by discussion and/or role play.
Timing: 30 minutes.

Process: Ask participants to make up three imaginary conversations consisting of:

1. Adult–Adult complementary transactions.
2. Parent–Parent complementary transactions.
3. Parent–Child complementary transactions.

These can then be role played by the group.

Crossed Transactions
In this type of transaction, the initiator is met with a response from an unexpected ego state.

MARY: Do you know where my diary is?
JANE: Don't you ever put anything away so that you know where to find it?
(Jane replies to Mary's Adult request from her Critical Parent.)

JEFFREY: These trainees think they know it all.
ADRIAN: Well, I've found this group very helpful and willing to learn.
(Adrian replies to Jeffrey's invitation to his Critical Parent with an Adult reaction.)

JONATHON: I'm feeling very low today.

KATHERINE: Oh! Pull yourself together—you're always whingeing about
    something.

*(Katherine's reply comes from her Critical Parent rather than the Nurturing Parent
that Jonathon was hoping for.)*

The diagrams would take the appearance of Figure 3.5.

Crossed transactions are ones in which the lines tracing them are not
parallel because the ego state which is addressed is not the one which
answers. When a transaction is crossed, a break in communication will

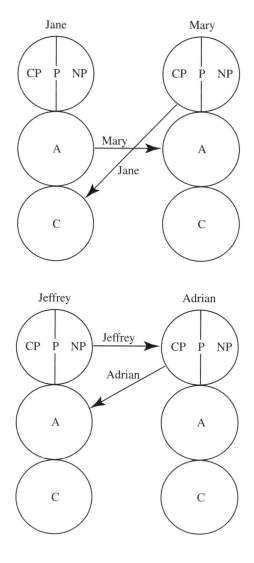

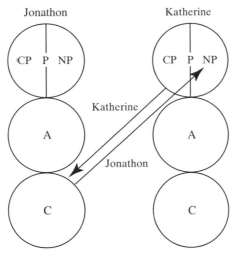

Figure 3.5: Crossed transactions

occur. One or both people will need to change ego states to allow the conversation to continue.

Exercise 3.10: Crossing the Transaction

Group Structure: Individual work followed by discussion and/or role play.
Timing: 30 minutes.

Process: Ask participants to make up examples of crossed transactions; for example, an Adult–Adult stimulus crossed by a Child–Parent response.

Variation: To give the group further practice, ask them to work in pairs. One person should start a conversation, the other should guess which ego state the person is demonstrating and answer from a different one.

Ulterior Transactions
The third basic kind of transaction is called ulterior because it involves hidden messages between ego states that are different from the surface or apparent one. In this example, Alice's manager is referring to a report which has been returned to Alice twice with several mistakes.

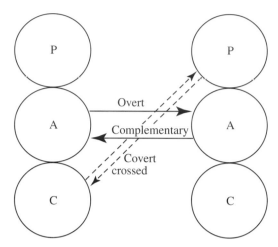

Figure 3.6: Ulterior transactions

MANAGER: Make this the last effort; it doesn't have to be perfect.
ALICE: I've nearly finished it.

This could be seen as Adult–Adult, but there is a hidden conversation going on:

MANAGER: *I'm going to have to put up with a second best; you've failed to meet my expectations.* (Parent)
ALICE: *This work is so boring; I'm fed up with it.* (Child)

The rule regarding ulterior transactions (Figure 3.6) is that the outcome of the communication will be determined at the psychological and not at the social level. Therefore, if there is a conflict at the psychological level, conflicts on the social level will not be resolved until the problem at the deeper level is addressed.

Exercise 3.11: Ulterior Transactions

Group Structure: Group work.
Timing: 10 minutes.
Materials: Copies of magazine advertisements.

Process: Analysing advertisements is a good way of understanding how ulterior/angular transactions work. Most advertisements, while apparently directed towards Adult (*Whizzo cleans your floor quicker and more efficiently*) are also aiming to hook Child or Parent (*You don't want to have dirtier floors than your neighbour, do you?*).

Provide the group with examples of magazine advertisements and give them time to work out the possible transactions.

Trainer Input

Let us now relate this to work in an organisation. We will do this at two levels—the personal and the organisational. We have already seen how organisations develop a culture which leads to an expectation of how people will behave.

Organisations have preferred or habitual communication patterns, just like people. Some organisations seem, for instance, to operate almost entirely from Critical Parent (Control) while others function more as Nurturing Parent (Care). If either of these ego states prevails, staff will tend to react from Free or Adapted Child, particularly when under stress. The way we feel about ourselves and others determines to a large extent the kinds of transaction we make.

Exercise 3.12: Organisation Ego States

Group Structure: Group brainstorm and discussion.
Timing: 10–15 minutes.

Process: Ask participants to brainstorm clues which might point to an organisation having developed a culture linked to a particular ego state: e.g.

CRITICAL PARENT

- Restrictive limits set on individual's behaviour
- Many rules and regulations
- Sanctions in force when rules broken
- Very tight hierarchy
- Vertical rather than horizontal channels of communication.

The next stage of this exercise could be to discuss advantages and disadvantages of each ego stage; how could the advantages of each be encouraged as part of the organisational culture?

Trainer Input

We have explored the ways in which individuals and organisations defend themselves against the anxiety which strong emotions can raise. These defence mechanisms help us to maintain the level of predictability which we need to keep feeling safe and in control of ourselves. It is probably true to say that we all, from time to time, feel anxious and/or depressed about the way our lives are going or about the world in general. However, if these feelings become overwhelming for a person and interfere with that person's functioning, he or she could be described as neurotic.

It is possible to describe certain styles of neuroses, both for individuals and for organisations. The psychoanalysts Kets de Vries and Miller (1984) identified five such patterns, listing their characteristics, the unconscious fantasy on which they are based and the dangers they could hold for an organisation.

PARANOID

The behaviour which characterises this style is mistrust and suspiciousness; hypersensitivity; constant searching for threat; overconcern with hidden motives and special meanings. The unconscious belief underlying this reaction could be expressed thus: 'There is no-one who I can really trust; I must be on my guard against the superior, menacing force which is out to get me.' The danger to the organisation in which this is the prevailing neurosis is that much energy is used in trying to confirm suspicions and fears. In this way reality is distorted and spontaneous action becomes unacceptable because it is too threatening to those caught up in the anxieties.

Compulsive

Here the neurotic aim is control through perfectionism. Characteristics include preoccupation with trivial details; everyone expected to conform; relationships seen in terms of dominance and submission; inability to relax; dogmatism. The unconscious belief is 'I don't want to be at the mercy of events; I have to master and control all the things affecting me' and the danger to an organisation is that this leads to extreme introspection: indecisiveness and postponement; avoidance due to the fear of making mistakes; inability to deviate from planned activity; excessive reliance on rules and a tendency not to be able to 'see the wood for the trees'.

Dramatic

Here it is self-dramatisation and the excessive expression of emotion which characterises the style. The atmosphere is one of excitement stemming from the narcissistic desire for attention. The fantasy belief is that 'I need to get attention and can't survive without it'. The main dangers are superficiality and an overdependence on intuition—taking action based entirely on feelings. Small events are dramatised and people can feel manipulated and used.

Depressive

Hopelessness and helplessness pervade this neurotic style leading to the feeling of being at the mercy of events with no ability or even right to control matters. The ability to think clearly is diminished, nothing seems stimulating or interesting and the pleasure has gone out of life. The belief being sustained is that 'I am just not worthy enough to change the course of events'. The danger is of an overly pessimistic outlook; difficulties in concentration and performance; passivity rather than action.

Schizoid

This is the most withdrawn style represented by detachment and lack of interest in day-to-day happenings or planning for the future. Indifference to praise or criticism. The unconscious fantasy is 'The world of reality does not offer any satisfaction; other people will eventually cause me problems so it is safer to remain distant'. This amount of emotional isolation causes frustration of dependency needs of others and can result in bewilderment and aggressiveness.

The best use of this kind of information is that it helps us describe the ways in which organisations, just like individuals, can get stuck in counter-productive patterns of reaction to the problems they face. However, like any labelling system, we should avoid the temptation to assume that this kind of stereotyping provides a solution. It doesn't, but it does provide us with a way of understanding what might be contributing to the difficulties.

Exercise 3.13: Recognising Patterns

Group Structure: Small discussion group work.
Timing: 30 minutes.

Process: Explain that recognition of a destructive pattern could lead to changes at a deeper level than might otherwise be the case. Maybe the problem has occurred because someone who is powerful in the hierarchy is caught in a neurotic pattern, and because this is an unconscious process, is unaware of the extreme nature of the behaviour. Or maybe the problem lies in the past history of the organisation; a neurotic culture may have been created, developed and is now handed on.

Set up small discussion groups and give them time to discuss any examples that they might have noticed in their own or in other organisations.

This completes our consideration of the influence of psychological processes at work in an organisation. By this time people will no doubt be thinking about changes to improve things. To effect change we need power and that is the focus of our next chapter.

REFERENCES

Berne, E. (1964). *Games People Play.* Penguin.

Berne, E. (1974). *What Do You Say After You've Said Hello!* Deutsch.

Freud, S. (1953–1974). *The Standard Edition of the Complete Psychological Works of Sigmund Freud* (J. Strachey, ed.). Hogarth.

Henderson, M. & Argyle, M. (1985). Social support by four categories of work colleagues; relationships between activities, stress and satisfaction. *Journal of Occupational Behaviour,* **6**: 229–39.

Kets de Vries, M.F.R & Miller, D. (1984). *The Neurotic Organisation; Diagnosing and Changing Counterproductive Styles of Management.* San Francisco: Jossey-Bass.

Maslow, A. (1970). *Motivation and Personality.* New York: Harper & Row.

Menzies, I.E.P. (1960). *Human Relations,* **13**: 95–121.

Stewart, I. & Joines, V. (1987). *TA Today.* Lifespace Publishing.

4

POWER AND POLITICS

People working in organisations often talk about feeling powerless. They might, for instance, see what improvements could be made to a particular system but feel blocked from making the necessary changes. This chapter presents training structures designed to enlighten people as to the nature of politics and power so that they can use their own personal power as constructively as possible for their own benefit and that of their organisation. We will explore power from the personal and organisational points of view. The first session provides a definition and an exploration of personal power.

SESSION 5: WHAT IS POWER?

Training Objectives

1. To define seven elements of personal power.
2. To provide participants with the opportunity to consider their own strengths and weaknesses.
3. To define seven types of organisational power.
4. To relate these to participants' personal experience.

Trainer Input

Politics and *power* are words often used as if they were interchangeable, but they do have different meanings. *The New Shorter Oxford Dictionary* (1993) definition of *power* includes 'Ability to act or affect something strongly; strength, might; vigour, energy; effectiveness . . .'.

Organisational politics has been described by Pfeffer (1981) as 'those activities taken within organisations to acquire, develop and use power and other resources to obtain one's preferred outcomes in a situation in which there is uncertainty about choices'.

A simpler comparison might be that power is the ability to effect change and politics is the use of power to get what you want!

Many people talk about feeling powerless in their organisation and it is true that most people are not able to influence their organisations to the extent that they would wish. However, it is also true that many people have more power than they think, and so the starting point for our session on power and politics is personal power. To be in as much control of your situation as possible, you need to develop confidence in your personal power. You can think of this kind of power as containing a number of elements.

- *Self-esteem:* This is your sense of your own value. It is based on the belief that you have a right to your place in the world. You are no more or no less important than anyone else.
- *Communication:* This is understanding and being understood. The ability to express yourself, whether in writing or speech, is vital whether you are negotiating a business deal or trying to resolve an interpersonal problem.
- *Knowledge:* This means finding out as much as you can about the facts of your situation. This might include knowledge of the history and its implications; knowing yourself and understanding your responses and motivation; understanding your rights and responsibilities.
- *Acceptance:* This means keeping a generally open, accepting and caring attitude towards people. There will, of course, be times when you find that you cannot accept the way some people behave and will respond appropriately. However, you have only to witness the effect of loving acceptance on an emotionally deprived child to understand the power of such acceptance.
- *Enthusiasm:* The capacity to experience a strong passionate commitment to a person, an idea or an activity releases a very potent energy. Those of you who have been taught something by an enthusiastic teacher will no doubt remember just how powerful a force that person's enthusiasm was.
- *Control:* The word *control* has a somewhat negative connotation. It suggests that someone is attempting to get what they want by pushing people around. However, the ability to influence others or one's environment is necessary from time to time. For instance, if you are a manager, you will probably need to exert some control in order to achieve your objectives and those of the organisation. However, do not be fooled into believing that the *only* way to be powerful is to learn how to push people around.
- *Transcendence.* You need to know when and how to rise above a situation you cannnot change. The skill is to know the difference between those things you cannot change and those you can. You cannot, for instance, change another person's behaviour—only the person can do that. You can give the person every opportunity to change, but if he or she chooses not to, you cannot do anything about it. You cannot change history; what happened in the past did happen. Practically speaking, all you can do is learn from the past and get on with the present.

These are the personal resources which contribute to your personal power. We each have strong points and areas that need building up. The ideal would be to have developed each element as much as possible. Try this exercise to help you to monitor your own personal power potential.

Exercise 4.1: Finding Your Personal Power

Group Structure: Individual followed by discussion in pairs.
Timing: 10 minutes for individual work, 10 minutes for discussion in pairs, can be followed by general group discussion.
Materials: Pen and paper for participants. Printed hand-out summary of input.

Process: Ask participants to write the headings of the seven elements down the left-hand side of their paper (or provide them with a prepared printed worksheet). Then ask them to think of a time when they felt very powerless. It could be a particular event, a particular time in their life, or when they are with a particular person. Next, ask them to think of a time when they have felt very powerful.

Suggest that it is possible to measure each of the elements on a scale 0–10 and ask them to give themselves a rating for each element in both of the situations.

Ask them to think about and discuss, in pairs: What conclusions can be drawn from the results? Which elements are strong points? Which need strengthening—and what practical measures could be taken as a beginning?

The next part of this session moves the focus from personal to organisational. Organisational power comes from various sources. French and Raven (1968) identified five main bases of power:

1. *Reward Power,* which derives from the ability to provide valued rewards to enhance status or increase resources.
2. *Coercive Power* stems from the capacity to produce fear in others through ability to apply sanctions such as demotion, salary cuts, suspension, dismissal and so on.
3. *Legitimate Power* comes from the willingness of others to accept someone's authority. Legitimate power can come through a role to which society attributes authority, e.g. police, doctor, judge, teacher and so on. It can also be assigned to someone by a person who already has legitimate power. For

example, a senior manager might delegate a junior manager to make certain decisions. Of course, legitimate power is only effective for as long as people accept being controlled by it; if the majority withdraw their support, the power ceases to exist.

4. *Referent Power* is held by people who inspire others by force of their personality. They are admired for their appearance, interpersonal skills or values. The obvious examples are entertainers, successful politicians or sports people.

5. *Expert Power* stems from being recognised as having superior skill or knowledge. Experts include professionals such as doctors, lawyers and co-workers who are seen as particularly skilful or knowledgeable in a particular field.

Robert Vecchio (1995) points out the distinctions to be drawn from among these five power bases. Expert and referent powers tend to be informal in nature, while legitimate, reward and coercive powers are more formal. Informal power has a greater capacity to affect employee's satisfaction and performance. Formal power, on the other hand, has potentially greater impact on immediate behaviour.

Although formal power can elicit a quick response, it will not necessarily produce agreement and commitment. If someone feels coerced, they may feel they have no choice but to co-operate at the time but their resentment may surface later. Apparently Machiavelli, the fifteenth-century Italian statesman, contended that people with formal power tend to remain in their positions of authority longer than those who rely on the informal sort. It seems likely, because expert and referent powers depend on people perceiving that the power exists. If this perception is blemished, the power diminishes. Idols turn out to have feet of clay; revered figures fall from their pedestals!

Informal power tends to reside in personal characteristics, whereas formal power resides more in the position the person holds.

Exercise 4.2: Who has Power over Who?

Group Structure: Individual followed by small groups.
Timing: 10–15 minutes in individual work; 30 minutes in small groups.
Materials: Worksheet: *Who has Power over Who?*; pens.

Process: Hand out worksheets explaining that the exercise is to examine several typical power relationships, each consisting of someone with authority and someone who is generally considered as a subordinate. The first example involves a teacher and student. On the 'teacher' line, tick the kind of power you think the teacher has over the student; on the 'student' line tick the power you feel the student might have over the teacher. Work down the list in a similar fashion.

When people have completed their worksheets, move them into pairs or small groups to discuss questions, such as: who do you think is the person with most power in each relationship? For each relationship, which type of power is the most significant? Can a power base be equally divided between each person?

WORKSHEET: WHO HAS POWER OVER WHO?

Relationship	Type of power				
	Leg	Rew	Coe	Ref	Exp
Teacher	. . . . . .	. . . . . .	. . . . . .	. . . . . .	. . . . . .
Student	. . . . . .	. . . . . .	. . . . . .	. . . . . .	. . . . . .
Shop Assistant	. . . . . .	. . . . . .	. . . . . .	. . . . . .	. . . . . .
Customer	. . . . . .	. . . . . .	. . . . . .	. . . . . .	. . . . . .
Counsellor	. . . . . .	. . . . . .	. . . . . .	. . . . . .	. . . . . .
Client	. . . . . .	. . . . . .	. . . . . .	. . . . . .	. . . . . .
Pop Star	. . . . . .	. . . . . .	. . . . . .	. . . . . .	. . . . . .
Fan	. . . . . .	. . . . . .	. . . . . .	. . . . . .	. . . . . .
Doctor	. . . . . .	. . . . . .	. . . . . .	. . . . . .	. . . . . .
Patient	. . . . . .	. . . . . .	. . . . . .	. . . . . .	. . . . . .
Manager	. . . . . .	. . . . . .	. . . . . .	. . . . . .	. . . . . .
Personal assistant	. . . . . .	. . . . . .	. . . . . .	. . . . . .	. . . . . .

Notes for the Trainer

This introduction to the concept of personal and organisational power could, for instance, act as an introductory session in a staff development or induction course for new managers or team leaders. One aim is to give people a realistic view of their own power. Frequently people are unaware of their own resources and importance, perceiving themselves as powerless. Others wildly overestimate their power base. The session could lead on to an exploration of rights and responsibilities of management and leadership roles or take a more personal turn focusing on personal power, perhaps encouraging participants to make personal action plans. We are using it here as the foundation for looking at the way organisational power structures can inhibit the meeting of objectives, particularly when associated with change.

SESSION 6: PYRAMID OF POWER

Training Objectives

1. To explore the implications of the power dynamics of hierarchical organisational structures.
2. To describe how 'communities-at-work' affect the power balance.
3. To provide an opportunity for participants to relate these ideas to their organisation and their practice.

Trainer Input

Organisations have existed ever since people got together to accomplish goals which they could not achieve alone. Any living organism which is not able to respond to its environment by changing will stagnate and eventually die; even the most successful organisation has to change in order to remain effective. Power is the capacity to bring about change, and in this session we will explore how organisational structure can hinder this process.

When groups come together this collective power has to be organised and directed towards the organisation's survival. Most organisations in our society structure the power in a hierarchy, which could be drawn as a pyramid—those people with most power to effect changes at the top and those with least at the bottom.

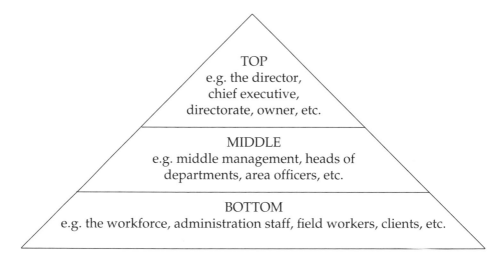

One of the ways in which we seek to fulfil our basic affiliation and safety needs (see Chapter 2, Session 2) is to create social groupings or communities. In these communities we can find people with whom to share interests, activities, perceptions; people who will in some way confirm the meaning of life that we have developed. These communities enable us to create some predictability in our life. Patterns of behaviour develop and there are rules about what is and is not acceptable behaviour. It is through our relationships in these groups that we seek to fulfil our needs for safety, predictability, affiliation, inclusion and acceptance.

Graeme Salaman (1986) points out that these communities exist among workers in an organisation, just as in other areas of life. Being part of such a community allows people to establish an element of their identity. They share a work-based morality (what things are and should be like; who are the heroes, heroines and villains and so on).

In these communities-at-work there is usually:

- a shared perception of the pattern of power distribution
- shared beliefs as to how power should be distributed
- some shared experience of mobility and/or life patterns, expectations, status, abilities, etc.
- the development of a recognisable shared culture in which people share the same world of meaning, language, jokes, knowledge of the world of work, jargon, and so on.

Exercise 4.3: Communities at Work

Group Structure: Individual work followed by discussion in small groups. Learning points drawn out in large group discussion.
Timing: Individual work: 10–15 minutes; small groups, 15 minutes.
Materials: Paper and coloured pens for participants

Process: Ask participants to list all the people with whom they have contact at work. Then ask them to make a chart representing how much contact they have with each person, perhaps using colours to denote different depths of contact. Suggest they note any subgroups or people who seem isolated.

The tension between the *need to change* in order to develop and the *resistance to change* because it threatens the secure system by which basic needs are being fulfilled, exists in individuals and in organisations.

Peter Marris (1986) writes about 'The Conservative Impulse' which he calls people's tendency to accept only those things which can be taken into their existing perceptual structure and avoid, reject or redefine anything that cannot be assimilated. In a very basic sense, our survival depends on our ability to predict events. The consequences of events are only predictable if they fit into the perception of the person who is interpreting them. The interpretations we make can only be understood in terms of our own purposes, preferences, antipathies and our learned experience of the world—what Eric Berne (1974) would call 'our life script'. Each of us handles the uncertainties of our lives by trying to conserve the fundamental structure of meaning we have developed for ourselves.

Any change causes some level of uncertainty. Change involves loss. It may be the loss of something immediately observable—for instance, the loss of a department, funding, piece of equipment, a person. It may be more difficult to define—for instance, an old machine might be replaced by a new one, which is better in any case, but for a while some people might sigh for the old, familiar machine. A new policy, say, on equal opportunities recruitment, with which everyone is in agreement, means the loss of former habitual practices. The reorientation period of thinking and feeling that is required in order to adapt to the change could be thought of as mourning.

Exercise 4.4: Loss and Change

Group Structure: Groups of 5–8 people.
Timing: 15 minutes in small groups followed by large group feedback.
Materials: A large sheet of flip chart paper and felt pen for each group.

Process: While they are in the small groups, ask participants to exchange information of changes (large or small) which they have experienced at work. They should then note down their responses under three headings on the large sheet of paper. The headings are *Thoughts*, *Feelings* and *Behaviour*.

These lists form the basis of the large group discussion.

Notes for the Trainer

This input and exercise are designed to raise awareness of the importance of acknowledging the profound effect of change on individuals in an organisation and the influence of the community at work. In his 1986 study of the London Fire Brigade's attempts to introduce an Equal Opportunities Policy, Graeme Salaman (1986) describes how the cohesiveness of the working community relationships inhibited the implementation of the change. In organisations where the process is not validated, it is the community-at-work which provides the safe and secure framework which the individual needs. Workplace communities can exert a very powerful force on the ability of an organisation to effect change successfully. This session makes a useful introduction to training about implementing and managing change in an organisation.

SESSION 7: THEM AND US

Training Objectives

1. To continue the exploration of the influence of communities on inter-personal and intergroup relationships.
2. To demonstrate the power dynamics of competition.
3. To increase awareness of feelings of 'insiders' and 'outsiders'.

Trainer Input

Because of the strength of the shared culture of the workshop community, it is easy for a 'them' and 'us' system to develop—in fact in some ways this is necessary in order for 'us' to be strong enough to survive. This exercise gives us an opportunity to explore this idea.

Exercise 4.5: 'Them' and 'Us'

Group Structure: Divide the large group into an equal number of small groups of about 6–10 members. You will need separate rooms for groups to use.
Timing: 45 minutes for group work, followed by large group feedback session.
Materials: Briefing sheets for each group.

Process: When the participants are in their small groups, hand out brief 1. When the 15 minutes are up, suggest that each person notes down any observations about the process of the group. Then hand out brief 2. Similarly, when that period is up, suggest they note down anything they notice and then hand each group brief 3.

When the groups have finished the exercise, they can reconvene and discuss questions such as:

- What factors helped or hindered coming to an agreement?
- Were there any differences in talking about themselves and talking about the other group?

- How did it feel to be the 'outsider' trying to persuade the other group?
- How did it feel to have an 'outsider' try to persuade you to change?
- Did any of the thoughts, feelings or behaviour you noticed in your-self and others bear a resemblance to your experiences in your organisation?

Brief 1: You have 15 minutes to think up a name for your group which you all agree represents your group.

Brief 2: Now you have 15 minutes to think up a name to represent the other group.

Brief 3: Send one of your group to another group to persuade them to accept the name you have chosen for them. You have 5 minutes to select your delegate and he or she will have 10 minutes to persuade the other group.

Notes for the Trainer

Although apparently very simple, this exercise can throw up deep feelings and important issues. For some people the experience of 'them' and 'us' is a distressingly personal aspect of their everyday lives; others might be shocked at how easy it can be to fall into predictable patterns of behaviour. You need to ensure that you leave enough time to process the exercise so that people can convert their experience into learning about working communities.

Trainer Input

Because of the strength of the shared culture of a workshop community, it is easy for a 'them' and 'us' system to develop—in fact in some ways it is actually necessary in order for 'us' to be strong enough to survive at all.

For instance, 'new' outsiders who make claims for status or power can be seen as competitive, impudent or expansionist. The existing 'older' group set out to prove that the claims of the 'new' group are illegitimate by accusing them of ignorance (*'They don't understand how things are here'*); inexperience (*'They'll learn in time'*); incompetence (*'They just haven't got what it takes'*); greed (*'They get paid three times what we did when we started so why aren't they satisfied?'*); youth (*'They're wet behind the ears!'*). Subgroups may arise as anyone supporting the claims gets criticised and is separated from the core 'older' group.

This older group seeks to create a comforting self-image by evolving a set of beliefs about itself which protects its skill- or power-base. (*'They don't make machines/cars/take the care/make films etc. etc. like they used to!'*) Selection, recruitment or training procedures which might have been fairly informal become more and more rigorous; 'protecting standards' becomes the watchword. Interestingly enough, these new standards are usually set by people who arrived at their positions through the original system!

The split between 'them' and 'us' becomes clearly identifiable; one group is concerned with keeping the power they have and the other with getting it. Let us now consider now how competition affects the picture.

Exercise 4.6: House of Cards

Group Structure: Minimum of 6 participants; maximum determined by space available.
Timing: One hour.
Materials: A pack of cards for each participant; sheets of newsprint or flip chart paper; felt-tipped markers; 'prizes' for one individual and one small group.

Process: *Stage 1:* Give the participants a pack of cards and ask them to silently estimate how many they could incorporate into a house of cards before the structure collapses. When each has made an estimate, ask them to build the houses of cards and discover whether they over- or underestimated their ability.

Stage 2: Now announce the second round and ask participants to dismantle the card-houses they made. Explain that now each person will publicly announce his or her goal and that each will be recorded for all to see. Tell them there will be a prize for the person with the highest estimate to complete the structure successfully.

Stage 3: When the winner has been determined and given a prize, form equal-sized teams of three or four people. This time, announce that the task will be to form three card-houses side by side. Announce that each team will now make an estimate and emphasise that teams should focus on a realistic goal. Tell the teams that there will be a prize for the highest estimate completed. As before, record the estimates before the teams begin building. When the winning team has been rewarded, the group meets together for discussion.

The discussion can focus around influences of competition on individual and group performance, group pressure, willingness to take risks, value of rewards and so on.

Variations: Instead of cards, other materials can be used: building blocks, dominoes, pins and straws, etc. Added pressure can be introduced by setting time limits on various phases of the exercise.

Trainer Input

Groups, like all living organisms, have strong survival instincts and will seek to influence organisation policy to their own advantage. Separate departments, for instance, struggle for their share of limited or new resources. Their rationale for allocation is more likely to be based on why it is for the good of the organisation for them to have this rather than their own need to survive.

Every organisation has to have a method of co-ordinating the variety of resources and functions needed to achieve its objectives—a system. Within the system, people, either individually or in their departments, define and pursue a range of goals.

These subgroups might create a special mystery around their job as a survival strategy. Elements might include jargon—a language which only they understand; special ways of doing things, special clothing, training and so on. A strong inclusion/exclusion structure is created, perhaps with control or limits on entry and the distribution of work.

Where the workforce is organised in distinct departments, it is not unusual for one not to know exactly what the other is doing. Mythology is created; 'The Training Department doesn't know what it's like to work in the field!'; 'Field workers don't understand the benefits of training!'. Strangely enough, even while people are saying these kinds of things, there might also be a resistance to attempts to bring different groups together to share their experiences. Complaints such as, 'These meetings are just a waste of time' or 'No "real work" gets done with all this talking' are heard; people find 'good' reasons for not attending or, if they do, appear bored or confused. Decisions which might be made somehow do not get implemented.

Managers of these departments can form their own community-at-work, which means that the majority of interdepartment communication takes place between them cutting out many opportunities for the staff to relate together.

Before we move on to the last part of this study of organisational power structures, let us take a moment to consider these last points.

Exercise 4.7: Discussion: Communities-at-Work in Competition

Group Structure: Individual work then whole group discussion.
Timing: 15–30 minutes

Process: Ask participants, either alone or in pairs, whether they can identify any behaviour or events in their organisation which demonstrate the points being made about the ways that the need to survive by accruing power can affect the dynamics of an organisation. Then bring the group together to discuss their observations.

Notes for the Trainer

This exploration of power dynamics is particularly useful in management training. Managers who are aware of these unconscious processes are much more likely to be able to make appropriate and constructive interventions if problems arise. The next input is based on Graeme Salaman's study mentioned earlier.

Trainer Input

People naturally relate to others with similar experience and perceptions, and so communities-at-work usually consist of people from the same horizontal level in the organisation. The problem for managers is that, if the organisation is small, there are not very many managers. Organisations which are structured into headquarters and a series of outposts usually have only one manager in each outpost. Graeme Salaman studied the process of the introduction of an Equal Opportunities Policy into the London Fire Brigade in the early 1980s. He found that one of the factors which hindered the success of that project was that each fire station had one Station Officer who was the first line manager. It goes without saying that in order to be effective, a first line manager needs to establish a co-operative relationship with the staff. Many do this by identifying with the culture of the group. For instance, they might choose to ignore minor contraventions of the rules like turning a blind eye to lateness or non-observation of safety procedures. This signals that the manager's loyalty is with the group rather than with 'head office'. This is one way they can become accepted as part of the community—'one of us'. The problem of 'turning a blind eye' to an Equal Opportunities Policy is that any compromise is discrimination. It is not possible to give someone half an equal opportunity in the same way as you can allow someone to be five minutes late!

Sometimes senior management will condone the culture and practices of informal groups in exchange for goodwill. Thus, first line managers can find themselves in an extremely difficult situation. Their job is to implement policies and they may find that they need to challenge some practices of the community-at-work in order to do this; their authority comes from the management line above in the pyramid and so they need to be supported by that line in order to be effective. However, a senior manager may decide that there will be less risk of conflict in supporting the community-at-work and so the first line manager's authority is diminished.

In this pyramid model, power is held at the top and distributed downwards. Power is increased by moving up the pyramid. The base of the pyramid is wider than the top, so there are fewer people at the top than at the bottom. Individuals who want to accrue power can only do so if space becomes available. This may happen by someone leaving or by new space being created. As people get higher up the pyramid, opportunities become fewer and so the only opportunity to accrue power may be to leave this pyramid for another one.

Not every organisation arranges its power this way. For instance, some groups decide to share their power equally by working collectively. However, these groups are also subject to the dynamics of the pyramid model. Firstly, they may be a discrete group in a hierarchical organisation and so the amount of power they have to distribute among themselves is limited. Secondly, they are functioning in a society which is organised on this model and so inevitably are affected by it.

Another way of accruing power is for individuals, who may be relatively powerless to effect change in an organisation by themselves, to unite around a shared belief, a recognised disadvantage or a shared need. Once a group is formed it becomes part of the structure and can communicate with the upper level. This kind of power can be perceived as a threat by those in the upper levels, since it is not following the predictable up-to-down power flow. It also breaks through the horizontal levels since people from all levels may identify with a particular group; for example, a women's group, a group for people with disability and so on.

To sum up, every organisation is made up of people, and people are motivated by a hierarchy of needs. Some basic needs are met by creating communities-at-work, where people can share their view of the world and receive support and recognition. Power (i.e. the capacity to effect change) in an organisation is usually held at the top of a pyramid and distributed downwards to the base. Resistance to change arises as a result of the impulse in each individual and group to survive by maintaining a predictable world.

Exercise 4.8: Power Pictures

Group Structure: Individual work followed by group discussion.
Timing: 10 minutes for individual work; 20 minutes for discussion.
Materials: Large sheet of paper; coloured pens for each participant.

Process: Ask participants to draw the shape of a large pyramid and to place the various levels of power they identify in their organisation. They should place themselves in the pyramid and mark the channels of communication which affect them.

Variation: Participants can draw their perception of the power dynamic in their organisation as it exists and as they would like it to be. This can lead to a discussion about ways to close the gap between what the position is now and what is desired.

This concludes the chapter on politics and power in organisations and Part I on understanding organisations. We move on in Part II to training structures designed to explore issues involved in working together.

REFERENCES

Berne, E. (1974). *What Do You Say After You Say Hello?* Andre Deutsch.

French, J.R. & Raven, B.H (1968). The bases of social power, in D. Cartwright & A. Zander (eds), *Group Dynamics*. New York: Harper & Row.

Marris, P. (1986). *Loss and Change.* Routledge & Kegan Paul.

New Shorter Oxford Dictionary, The (1993). Clarendon Press.

Pfeffer, J. (1981). *Power in Organisations*. Boston: Pitman Publishing Co.

Salaman, G. (1986) *Working*. Ellis Horwood Ltd & Tavistock Publications.

Vecchio, R.P (1995). *Organizational Behaviour* (3rd edition). The Dryden Press, Harcourt Brace College Publishers.

II

WORKING TOGETHER

5

DEVELOPING THE TEAM

So far we have concentrated on problems people may experience as a result of the type of organisation in which they find themselves. However, for some people the problems are caused, not so much by the organisation but by the people with whom they find themselves working. In the same way that we cannot choose our relatives, most of us cannot choose our fellow workers and so, as with our relatives, we have to find a way of getting on with them at least well enough to maintain the relationship we need.

Part II deals with some of the issues which arise for people who are members or leaders of a team. These include training structures to help people explore the roles and responsibilities of a team leader. We also look at different ways of working constructively to resolve conflict and consider issues related to being in charge of others whether as a manager, supervisor, trainer or coach.

SESSION 8: BEING IN A TEAM

Training Objectives

1. To define terms: *group, team, teamwork*.
2. To identify advantages and disadvantages of working in a team.
3. To use Schutz's theory of group development to consider how personal needs affect team membership.
4. To describe a team life-cycle.
5. To introduce a diagnostic framework for team problems.

Trainer Input

In this session, we will be exploring some of the issues which relate to working in a team. Firstly, let's be clear what we mean when we talk about a team. We all know something about groups because it would be difficult to live and work in this society without having some experience of them.

Exercise 5.1: How Many Groups?

Group Structure: Brainstorm.
Materials: Flip chart and pen for trainer.
Timing: 5 minutes.

Process: Ask group to call out the groups of which they are or have been a member. The idea is to get as large a range as possible: family, school classes, choirs, football teams, art classes and so on.

One of the groups to which we belong is our work team. What is it that makes this different from all these other groups we have mentioned? Alison Hardingham (1995) suggests that the key question to ask when you are trying to decide whether your work group is a team or not is: 'Do all the members of my group share at least one goal that can be accomplished only through the joint efforts of us all?' If the answer is 'Yes', you are the member of a team. The need to work together to meet shared goals makes the difference between a team and a group. This means that there are particular requirements, benefits and costs which come with being a team. For instance, goals need to be understood in the same way by everyone in the team and we have already seen in the previous section how people can have very different perceptions and aims.

Exercise 5.2: Pros and Cons

Group Structure: Two groups of about 6–8 people (more groups if the number of participants is too large).
Timing: 10 minutes in groups; 20 minutes for whole group discussion.

Process: Brief one group to work together to identify all the disadvantages they can think of regarding working in a team. The other group will make a similar list of all the advantages they can think of.

When the groups come together, ask someone from each group to present their list and invite other participants to add any items they can think of.

Trainer Input

Some of you might be feeling that the disadvantages you have identified might make it better to avoid teams altogether—that the costs outweigh the benefits. Let's take a look at the pros and cons. The most commonly identified disadvantages of teamwork can come under these headings:

- Things can take a long time if too much time and energy is spent in communication; too much talk and not enough action!
- Bad relationships between people can seriously affect the quality of work.
- The organisation as a whole can suffer if individual teams become very competitive.

However potentially serious these problems are, there are advantages to teamwork, such as:

- For many people, working with other people releases energy and creativity. The more brains working on a problem, the more likely a solution. Different perspectives and suggestions can spark off creative solutions.
- Working with people can be very satisfying; people are social beings and the structure of the team allows for personal space and development, which most of us need in order to blossom.
- Teamwork can be efficient. A larger pool of skills and experience is available and, together, people can create systems which make the best use of their time and energy.

We should also remember that sometimes there is no choice; some things can only be achieved through teamwork. We will spend the rest of this session considering some of the underlying causes for possible problems.

Group Life-cycle
Let's look at one idea about the life-cycle of a group. Tuckman and Jenson's (1977) theory that groups pass through a process of development will help us understand what might be happening in our teams.

Forming
This starts when people get together for the first time. Their energy is mostly taken up with finding out who everyone is and what the ground rules are. If you were observing a group in this stage you would notice people being extremely polite, perhaps even embarrassed. Communication would be very stilted; if there was a leader, most communication would be directed towards him or her. Although a lot of enthusiasm would be expressed, in fact not very much work gets done. The key issues at the forming stage are cohesion and involvement.

Storming

The next stage often feels like a time of conflict; members bargain with each other as they try to sort out what each of them, individually and as members of the team, wants out of the process. People might reveal their personal goals and some hostility might be expressed as differences might be revealed. It is a time of lively debate and discussion, although often the issues remain unresolved. Power battles can be fought as people either try to take control or resist control. Key issues are group direction and the management of conflict.

Norming

This happens when members of the group develop ways of working together and closer relationships. The conflicts of the previous stage are resolved and the questions of who will do what and how it will be done are addressed. Working rules are established and a framework of communication established.

Performing

The next stage, performing, is concerned with actually getting on with the work. At this stage the team could be said to be mature with an atmosphere of relaxed, purposeful confidence. Communication is mostly about the work and goals are achieved. Groups which make little progress in the previous stages find it difficult to get to this point.

Adjourning

This is the final, ending stage of the group. It disbands, either because the task has been achieved or because members have left. The energy of the group is taken up with tying up loose ends and planning for the future. There may be feelings of sadness as people say goodbye as well as celebrations of achievements.

Exercise 5.3: Group Life-cycles

Group Structure: Individual work followed by small discussion groups.
Timing: 15 minutes.

Process: Ask people to think of a group of which they are, or have been, a member and in which there have been some problems. Giving them the previous life-cycle plan, ask them to try to assess which phase the group is in and what might be necessary to move it forward.

Variation: Participants can be asked to identify which phase their present work team has reached.

Individual Needs

William Schutz (1966) offers an idea about individual needs in a group, which helps us understand the process of this life-cycle. He felt that people came to the group with three important individual psychological needs: inclusion, control and affection.

Inclusion

This is the need we all have to some extent to feel included, to be noticed and accepted, to get the attention and recognition we feel we deserve. Getting this need met will dominate the behaviour of people with high inclusion needs. For instance, the time people spend preparing for a group is often related to their inclusion needs. Deciding what clothes to wear, learning the group's rules in advance, joining with a friend, are all ways of trying to ensure inclusion.

Time is often spent at the beginning of a group dealing with inclusion and exclusion issues. This, of course, connects to the 'forming' stage discussed above. There is very little risk-taking at this stage and people probably feel at their most self-conscious.

Control

This is our need to be clear about who can control us and who we can control. Just as some people have high inclusion needs, some have high control needs. What seems to happen is that when inclusion needs have been met sufficiently for enough people, the control need makes itself felt. This is when individuals are most likely to be in conflict—the 'storming' stage that Tuckman and Jensen identified. If and when an acceptable balance of control is worked out, the third set of needs comes into play.

Affection

This is the stage when people develop stronger emotional attachments between themselves, which may turn out to be either fleeting or long-term alliances or friendships.

The particular mix of inclusion, control and affection needs present in a group determines the underlying dynamics—the process.

Exercise 5.4: Life in This Group

Group Structure: Individual worksheets, then group discussion.
Materials: Questionnaire worksheet for each participant.
Timing: 10 minutes to complete questionnaire; 20 minutes for discussion.

GROUP LIFE WORKSHEET

Please spend a few minutes jotting down your answers to these questions. Although they relate to your experience of being a member of this particular group, you might find it interesting to note whether any of your answers would relate to other groups of which you are a member.

1. What kind of person do you want to be in this group? e.g. How do you want to be seen by others? How would you like to think of yourself? What roles do you find yourself playing? What roles do you want to play? What kind of preparations do you make before meeting?
2. How far do you feel liked and accepted in the group? Do you like and accept all, some or none of the other members?
3. How far do you feel you are able to control and influence others in the group?
4. How far do you feel controlled by others?
5. Do you feel liked and accepted in the group? Do you like and accept all, some or none of the other members?
6. Do you feel particularly close to some of the group? Have you noticed people making friendships?

What all this means is that when a group or team are together there are two agendas. One is related to the actual work or task to be done—you could call this the agenda *on* the table; the other is about the personal issues we have just described—this is the agenda *under* the table. If there are unresolved issues on the agenda under the table, conflicts will probably continue to arise which affect the agenda on the table.

We each have various ways of coping with needs which are unmet. Some people become very tough and try to control people into meeting their needs. They might engage in arguing, bullying or ignoring others. They try to control matters by setting up very strict procedures and ordering others about. They will resist the authority of anyone else.

Some people have a more tender approach. They form alliances or subgroups. They will avoid conflict by whatever means they can, being ultra helpful and covering over divisions. They will look for people to support, and people to support them.

The third option is to withdraw from the problem. These are the people who sit back displaying indifference and leaving others to fight it out. They will deny the existence of tension or feelings, appealing to logic and facts.

Exercise 5.5: Coping Mechanisms

Group Structure: Whole group take part in a problem-solving exercise then break into small discussion groups.
Timing: 30 minutes for task; 20 minutes discussion in small groups; 10 minutes in large group to draw learning points together.
Materials: Briefing sheet; questionnaire for each participant.

Process: Explain to the group that they have 30 minutes to solve the problem you will give them. Tell them that you will take no further part in the exercise other than to tell them when the time is up. Lay the sheet on the floor and withdraw from the group to an observer's position.

When time is up, ask people to fill in the questionnaire and then split into small groups to discuss their observations. The main point is to try to identify what personal needs might underlie some of the reactions of participants during the exercise.

BRIEFING SHEET
Spend 10 minutes on your own working on the following problem:

A fly is in a top corner of a square room that measures 24 feet on a side and is 8 feet high. It sees an edible crumb at the opposite bottom corner. The fly wants to reach the crumb over the shortest possible path. How long is the path?

When the 10 minutes are over, make sure that everyone in the group understands and agrees upon the answer.

Variation: You can substitute any task which has a degree of difficulty for the group. The idea is to provide them with something which will create pressure.

QUESTIONNAIRE
While the exercise was going on did you notice yourself or others engaging in the following behaviour:

- Arguing, ridiculing, ignoring others, controlling the group, ordering others about, resisting authority?
- Forming alliances and subgroups, avoiding conflict, looking for others to support, being ultra helpful, trying to smother any divisions?
- Sitting back, showing indifference, leaving others to fight it out, denying existence of tension or feelings, appealing to logic, wanting to 'stick to the facts'?

In general terms, how effective were these strategies in solving whatever the problem was at the time?

Notes for the Trainer

Obviously the point of this exercise is to create a situation where, because they feel under pressure, people resort to their habitual coping mechanisms. You will probably notice some of these while you are observing and might want to feed them back into the general discussion if the participants themselves have

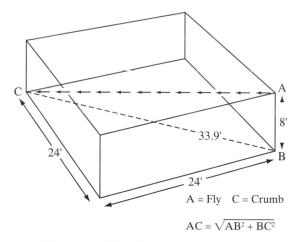

$$AC = \sqrt{AB^2 + BC^2}$$

Figure 5.1: The shortest path to the crumb

not noticed them. You can move the discussion into suggesting participants identify any behaviour that cropped up in the exercise which they also recognise in their work team.

Incidentally, the answer is 35 ft (actually 34.8 ft). It requires two calculations of the Pythagoras theorem: (1) find the diagonal of the room; (2) this dimension and the height of the wall provide the two sides necessary to find the shortest distance.

Trainer Input

Having experienced some of the problems associated with not getting our psychological needs met, we can think about what behaviours are most likely to help the team to deal constructively with the various problems that are bound to arise. These can be split into two types: one to do with helping the task in hand to be completed, and the other to do with maintaining the general atmosphere in the team.

- *Task.* The behaviours which are most likely to assist a team to work together constructively are initiating, opinion seeking, information seeking, information giving, clarifying, elaborating, summarising and consensus testing.
- *Maintenance.* The behaviours most likely to keep the general atmosphere one which is conducive to co-operative problem-solving are harmonising, compromising, gatekeeping, accepting, encouraging, diagnosing and standard setting and testing.

Very often these are seen as the function of the manager or team leader although they can be undertaken by any member.

Exercise 5.6: Problem-solving Mechanisms

Group Structure: Individual work followed by small or large group discussion.
Materials: List of problem solving behaviours for each participant.
Timing: 5 minutes to fill in questionnaire; 15 minutes for discussion.

Process: Ask group to think back to the previous exercise and to tick each of the behaviours they noticed, together with the name(s) of the person they noticed carrying out the functions.

QUESTIONNAIRE: Problem-solving Behaviours

. . . . . *Initiating:* e.g. 'Let's try . . .'; 'I think the answer is . . .'.
. . . . . *Opinion seeking:* e.g. 'What does everyone think about this?'.
. . . . . *Information seeking:* e.g. 'Is anyone here good at maths?'.
. . . . . *Information giving:* e.g. 'I know about geometry'.
. . . . . *Clarifying:* e.g. 'We could draw a plan of this'.
. . . . . *Elaborating:* e.g. 'I agree with Jane's idea and think we could take it
          further by . . .'.
. . . . . *Summarising:* e.g. 'So far, we've had the following ideas'.
. . . . . *Consensus taking:* e.g. 'Let's hear what everyone thinks'.
. . . . . *Harmonising:* e.g. 'You could both be right'.
. . . . . *Compromising:* e.g. 'You seem to know more about this than me'.
. . . . . *Gatekeeping:* e.g. 'Let's talk one at a time'.
. . . . . *Accepting:* e.g. 'You're a good team to work with'.
. . . . . *Encouraging:* e.g. 'I know not everyone is good at maths but we can
          all have a go at this'.
. . . . . *Diagnosing:* e.g. 'I think the nature of the problem is . . .'.
. . . . . *Standard setting/testing:* e.g. 'Let's just check our answer'.

Tick any of the behaviours that you noticed in the previous exercise and put the name of the person(s) carrying them out if you can.

Notes for the Trainer

This session has dealt with some of the dynamics which may be affecting participant's work teams. Its purpose is to help them understand what might be going wrong if they are experiencing problems. The following session can act as an introduction to a longer course on team-building or stand on its own as a unit of a management training course. The first exercise gives participants the chance to think creatively about their team.

SESSION 9: UNDERSTANDING TEAM PROBLEMS

Training Objectives

1. To apply the theory in the previous session.
2. To use a creative approach to analysing the team.
3. To provide a diagnostic framework for team problems.

Exercise 5.7: My Team Is . . .

Group Structure: Individual work followed by discussion.
Timing: 20 minutes.
Materials: Hand-out questionnaire.

Process: Provide everyone with a questionnaire and give them time to complete it either with words or images. The results can be shared in the group and can lead to a discussion about the nature of the teams of which people are members.

MY TEAM IS . . .

Complete each of these sentences with a phrase or sketch; put down whatever comes into your mind first and do not worry too much about making sense of it!

If my team was a family it would be:

If my team was a school it would be:

If my team was a play it would be:

If my team was an animal it would be:

If my team was a sport it would be:

The following exercise can lead on to further course work or be used by participants as a trigger to making desired changes.

Exercise 5.8: What's Wrong with the Team?

Group Structure: Individual questionnaire which could lead to group discussions or problems solving groups.
Timing: 15 minutes to complete questionnaire plus discussion or group work.
Materials: Questionnaire for each participant.

Process: Give out the questionnaires and ask participants to answer the questions as honestly as they can. Point out that they may wish to keep some of their answers confidential when it comes to discussion time. These are matters to which they may want to give more thought.

The questionnaire is a diagnostic tool for identifying possible causes of problems.

WHAT'S WRONG WITH THE TEAM?
DIAGNOSTIC QUESTIONNAIRE

Setting Objectives
- What is the overall purpose of the team?
- How does the team fit into the organisation?
- What does it do?
- What doesn't it do?
- What are its priorities?
- What external influences does it need to respond to?
- What should change as a result of the team's success?
- What is the best that this team could achieve?
- What are the consequences of failure?

Achieving Objectives
- Generally, how well is the team achieving its objectives?
- Which objectives have been met?
- What helped or hindered your success?
- Which objectives haven't been met?
- What helped or hindered progress?
- What changes do you think would improve chances of meeting those objectives yet to be achieved?
- What might happen in the future to help or hinder progress?
- Do you think the team would be able to overcome future obstacles? How?
- What are you most pleased with about the team's achievements?
- What are you most concerned about regarding the team's achievements so far?

Team Dynamics
- Do you enjoy working in this team?
- What do you like most about it?
- What do you like least?
- What changes would make things better for you?
- What annoys you most about the team?
- What pleases you most?
- Have your feelings about the team changed over time? How? Why?
- Do you have any reason for wanting to leave the team?
- Are there any members of the team you particularly dislike working with? Why?
- Are there any members you particularly like working with? Why?
- Do you feel valued as a member of the team? If not, why not?

This chapter has focused on issues concerned with team building; we will continue this exploration in the next chapter by considering the various roles and responsibilities of team members.

REFERENCES

Hardingham, A. (1995). *Working in Teams.* Institute of Personnel & Development.
Schultz, W. (1966). *The Interpersonal Underworld.* Science Behaviour Books.
Tuckman, B. & Jenson, N. (1977). Stages of small group development revisited, *Group and Organisational Studies*, 2: 419–27.

6

ROLES AND RESPONSIBILITIES

This chapter continues the exploration of problems which can arise through working together. In order for a team to be successful, various functions have to be fulfilled and the first training session focuses on this. The second session in this chapter looks specifically at the role of leader.

SESSION 10: GROUP ROLES

Training Objectives:

1. To introduce Belbin's (1981) idea of the eight major roles necessary for an effective working team.
2. To explore the functions of these roles.
3. To consider problems which might arise if they are not carried out.

Trainer Input

Meredith Belbin in the 1980s conducted a study of different management teams in an attempt to identify the team roles which contributed most to effective team working. This study is very well known now and is often used as an analysis tool for measuring a team's effectiveness. Alison Hardingham's (1995) consultancy has developed descriptions of the roles as follows:

Chairperson/co-ordinator: The person who fulfils this role keeps the team clear about its objectives and sets the agenda. Although not necessarily the most brilliant member of the team, he or she is stable, dominant and extrovert. The 'chairperson' usually presides over group meetings adopting a relaxed and non-aggressive style and is seen as the social leader.

Shaper: This person is a direction setter. Also usually an extrovert bringing a great deal of energy to the team. He or she is quick to challenge and quick to respond to challenges; one of the dominant members of the team who sees the team as an extension of his or her ego, shaping the team's efforts.

Plant: This is the creative thinker in the team, with a high IQ able to 'scatter seeds' for others to nourish. This is the person most likely to search for original approaches, an original and radical thinker. On the more negative side, he or she may not take criticism of ideas well, perhaps taking offence or sulking.

Monitor-evaluator: This is a critical thinker, also with a high IQ but with a serious, measured approach. Has the ability to make a dispassionate analysis of the situation. Not such an original thinker but will stop the team from committing itself to a misguided project. His or her best skills include assimilating, interpreting and evaluating large volumes of complex written material. On the downside this person can lower a team's morale by dampening enthusiasm at the wrong time.

Implementer: The main skill of this person lies in turning ideas into manageable tasks. This is someone who is stable, controlled and practical, not easily deflated or discouraged. This person will work to produce a stable structure where he or she feels most comfortable. The implementer may be thrown by sudden changes of plan.

Teamworker: This is the most sensitive member of the team, the person most aware of individual needs and worries. This is a good listener and a popular smoother of people's feelings. He or she puts the maintenance of good relationships high on the priority list, but probably, as a result, is not too good at facing and dealing with conflict.

Completer-finisher: This person keeps the team on its toes and is only really at ease when every detail has been personally checked. Introverted and rather anxious, he or she can be impatient and intolerant of people who have a more casual approach. Can be bogged down in detail.

Resource investigator: This person is the channel of communication with the 'outside world', with masses of outside contacts. He or she is likely to have a relaxed and sociable style, although lacking the personal originality of the 'Plant'. He or she preserves the team from stagnation and from losing touch with the outside world.

Specialist: This person has a high degree of expertise in his or her own field and can sometimes make his or her own rules. This person's skill and experience adds significantly to the capability of the team but they can remain narrowly focused on his/her own knowledge or skill base and can appear uninterested in people or other team issues.

Notes for the Trainer

There are many exercises devised to show the way that people can act together when they are in a team. They are usually set up as a problem-solving exercise based on some crisis situation in which people have to work together to come to a decision. The most important aspect of such an exercise is the feedback when people share their observations about their own behaviour and that of others.

Here is an example of an exercise which can be used to heighten people's awareness of the way that roles develop in a team, i.e. a group with a task and shared objectives.

Exercise 6.1: The Flood

Group Structure: Individual worksheet followed by small group work and group discussion.
Timing: One to one-and-a-half hours.
Materials: Worksheet for each person. If possible provide a separate room for each working group. Two sheets of notepaper and pen for each small group.

Process: Explain that participants will be making a decision about what things might be most important to them in an emergency situation. Give out the sheets and give people 1 or 2 minutes to read them. Then give them 5 minutes in which they have to choose their five most important items.

When everyone has done this, divide into groups of four or five and give each group 15 minutes to decide collectively on the five most important items.

Ask each small group to nominate a spokesperson. Bring the whole group together and ask the spokespeople to make a small group in the centre. The task of the spokespeople is to try to reach a consensus for the whole group. The communication rules are:

1. People in the small groups can talk to each other and can, of course, hear what the group in the centre is saying.
2. Members of the small group can only communicate with their spokesperson via written notes.
3. A small group can only pass two notes to their spokesperson during the whole exercise.

The small group will work in the centre for 15 minutes.

At the end of the exercise bring the group together for a discussion which can be focused on their observations of the roles being played. Who took which role? Which roles seemed most helpful? Were there any roles which hindered the decision making? . . . and so on.

THE FLOOD WORKSHEET

You have been on a trip abroad. You arrive home to discover that it has been raining in torrents for four days and that the area where you live is under a flood warning. As you arrive, your street is being evacuated as a flood seems imminent. You explain the situation to the police and fire officers who are managing the evacuation and ask for a couple of minutes to go into your home and collect some of your precious things. They reluctantly allow you five minutes and say that you can only take five things because space is so limited. Which of the five following items would you save?

1. A picture you have been working on for several weeks which you intend to enter for an exhibition.
2. Your only photograph of your parents when they were young.
3. Your diary.
4. A computer disk containing important material which you would have difficulty in rewriting.
5. The first drawing your child brought home from school.
6. A video of your wedding or some other important family occasion.
7. Your favourite scarf, which was given to you as a gift by a dear friend.
8. Your collection of love-letters.
9. A bottle from your collection of very old and very special wine.
10. A very expensive art book which you have borrowed from a friend.
11. The £1,000 in cash you have hidden in case of emergency.
12. A photograph album containing photographs of people who are no longer alive.
13. Your jewellery case.
14. The kitchen knife which is the only one you ever use and which you have had for a long time.
15. A patchwork quilt which you spent many months making and which has pride of place in your bedroom.
16. An indoor plant which you have put a great deal of effort into raising and keeping and which is just beginning to flourish.
17. Your favourite very comfortable pair of shoes.
18. A sculpture you made when you were at school, for which you won a prize.
19. A piece of porcelain handed down as a family heirloom, through your great grandmother, grandmother, mother and now you.

20. The accounts which you have just finished doing as treasurer of a
    local organisation to which you belong.

Remember: **Whatever you leave behind is likely to be ruined by the
flood. You have 5 minutes to choose.**

Notes for the Trainer

Unlike some similar exercises, there is no 'right' answer to this; each person
has his or her own particular values. The session with the spokespeople points
up the problems of representing other people accurately and fairly.

SESSION 11: THE ROLE OF LEADER

Training Objectives

1. To define what leadership is and what it is not.
2. To list qualities of a good leader
3. To explore responsibilities of a leader
4. To present a Transactional Analysis view of leadership functions.

Trainer Input

We have considered the roles and functions which are necessary for a team to
be successful. In this session we will focus on just one role; that of the leader.
A lot does depend on the quality of the leadership a team receives.

Exercise 6.2: What is Leadership? What isn't it?

Group Structure: Brainstorm.
Timing: 5 minutes.

Process: Write at the top of a flip chart 'A leader is . . . ' and ask people to
call out how they would end the sentence, writing down the list as they
do so. Then write 'A leader is not . . . ' and make a similar list.

Many of us tend to believe that the word 'leader' means one person
dominating another, but as we can see through the work we have done so far

Figure 6.1: Adair's three functions of leadership

the role of leader is far more complex than forcing people to do what you tell them. John Adair (1987), who has written a great deal about effective management, suggests that people do not actually choose or accept domineering individuals as leaders, except in obvious situations such as prison. Physical strength or size, a dominant personality or a will for power over others, is not the answer. In any situation where people need to co-operate, effective leadership is founded upon respect and trust, not fear and submission.

In the context of teamwork, leadership involves focusing the efforts of a group of people towards a common goal and enabling them to work together as a team.

An important aspect of leadership is knowing yourself. Knowing your own strengths and weaknesses is a key step on the path of making the most of what you have to offer. For one thing, if you are clear about your strengths and weaknesses you can ensure that you select team workers who can compensate for what you lack. You could deliberately choose people who have strengths, knowledge and experience which you do not possess.

Adair explains the functions of leadership as three overlapping areas: achieving the task, developing the individual, and building and maintaining the team (Figure 6.1).

Certain key functions are necessary in order to fulfil the three circles of responsibility. This does not mean that a leader has to do everything, but he or she is accountable for the three roles.

Exercise 6.3: Three Functions of Leadership

Group Structure: Small groups followed by discussion.
Timing: 30 minutes.
Materials: Prepare in advance a large sheet of paper for each small group.

Each sheet should have the three headings: ACHIEVING THE TASK; BUILDING AND MAINTAINING THE TEAM; DEVELOPING THE INDIVIDUAL.

Process: Ask each group to make a list of the questions a leader could ask of himself or herself to ensure that the important elements of each function were being covered.

When groups have finished, compare the lists and discuss any observations. You could then hand out the following list for comparison—or add in any which the groups seemed to have missed from their own list.

These are the questions which seem to be most useful:

Task:
- Do I understand the task?
- What are my particular responsibilities?
- Are the objectives agreed with my manager?
- Do the working conditions provide what is necessary for success?
- Are the resources adequate?
- Do I, or any others involved, need extra training?
- Am I sure of the priorities?
- Am I regularly checking progress?
- Who will cover for me if I am absent?

Maintaining the Team
- Does the team understand and accept the objectives?
- Do they know what standard of performance is expected?
- Do they understand health and safety requirements?
- Is the team the correct size for the job?
- How are the team getting on together?
- Is there a good team spirit?
- Are team members accepting the structure of discipline?
- How do I deal with infringements?
- How are grievances dealt with?
- Is the team consulted often enough?
- Are briefings effective?
- How am I supporting individuals and the team as a whole?

Developing the Individual
- Has each person agreed targets?
- Does each person know the other team members and organisation well enough?

- Has each person got an accurate and clearly understood job description?
- Can I delegate more to individuals?
- Has adequate provision for training been made for each person?
- Is individual performance regularly reviewed?
- Is there any person who is in the wrong job for his or her particular mix of skills and experience?
- Do I spend time listening, developing and counselling each person?
- Do I know how different each person is from the others?
- Does each person have the necessary knowledge about pensions, redundancy and so on?
- Are regular appraisal sessions held?

One of the most important responsibilities of leadership is to define your objectives; until you know clearly what you want you cannot begin to direct others towards the goal. If you were on a journey, would you follow someone who didn't know where he or she was going?

Gerard Egan (1982) has laid out a very clear scheme for ensuring that goals are set effectively. Good targets should be clear and specific; measurable or verifiable; time bounded; realistic in terms of available resources; adequate to contribute in a substantial way towards the aim; and in keeping with organisational and personal values.

Exercise 6.4: Setting Goals

Group Structure: Individual or seminar work followed by discussion.
Timing: 30–45 minutes.
Materials: Brief scenarios printed on individual cards to give to individuals or seminar groups. The scenarios should relate to the kind of work in which course participants are engaged.

Process: Hand out the scenarios to individuals or seminar groups asking them to come up with a set of goals for each problem. The goals must be tested against the above criteria.

Group discussion should focus more on the difficulties or advantages of the process of goal setting than on the content of the problems.

Once the team have agreed their task objectives, it is the turn of the individual. Each person needs a clear personal objective or target. These targets ideally should be worked out with the person involved so that everyone feels a personal commitment to the team goals.

Exercise 6.5: Personal Goals

Group Structure: Individual work followed by discussion.
Timing: 20 minutes.

Process: Suggest that participants select one area of their own work where they would like to initiate some change and ask them to spend about 10 minutes devising at least one goal which would move them onwards.

Then ask them to find a partner and share the goals with each other. The main task of the partner is to check whether the goals fit the criteria.

Variation: An interesting addition to the exercise is to ask participants to make an arrangement to contact their partner in, say, a month's time when they can check how the goals are progressing. Make sure that people actually take out their diaries and arrange a specific time when they will make contact.

Exercise 6.6: Roles and Responsibilities of Leadership

Group Structure: Seminar groups.
Timing: 45 minutes.
Materials: Worksheet for each group.

Process: Give each seminar group a worksheet which lists six functions of leadership and ask them to list behaviours which go with each function.

WORKSHEET: WHAT WOULD A GOOD LEADER BE DOING?
This is a list of the general functions required of a leader. Write, beside each one, a list of examples of leader behaviours which go with each function:

Planning:

Initiating:

Controlling:

Supporting:

Informing:

Evaluating:

Examples might include:

Planning: Seeking all available information; defining group task, purpose or goal; creating a workable plan.

Initiating: Briefing group on aims and plan; explaining why aim or plan is necessary; allocating tasks to group members, setting group standards.

Controlling: Maintaining group standards; influencing tempo, ensuring all actions are taken towards objectives; keeping discussions on track; moving group to action or decision.

Supporting: Expressing acceptance of individuals and their efforts; encouraging or counselling people; constructively disciplining group or individuals; creating team spirit; relieving tension with humour; reconciling disagreements or getting others to explore them.

Informing: Clarifying task and plan; giving new information if necessary; receiving information from the group; summarising suggestions and ideas clearly.

Evaluating: Checking feasibility of an idea; testing the consequences of a proposed solution; evaluating group performance; helping the group to evaluate its own performance against standards.

Notes for the Trainer

The last section of this session returns to Transactional Analysis which offers an interesting model for managing or leading others. You may have already introduced your training participants to the TA concept of ego states (see Chapter 2), in which case you will not need to give the explanatory introduction which follows.

Trainer Input

According to Transactional Analysis, every personality has three sets of programming or ego states: Parent, Adult and Child. The idea is that individual behaviour during transactions with another person is determined by the particular ego state in action at the time. There are many factors which could determine which ego state is activated—early life experiences, the circumstances surrounding the transaction as well, of course, as the other person's ego state. The ego state with which we are concerned now is the Parent.

This is the part of the personality containing all the instructions and guidance—the *shoulds, oughts, dos* and *don'ts*—that we acquired through intimate association with our parents and other authority figures in our youth.

The Parent ego state has two sides. Various Transactional analysts have referred to them as the Nurturing Parent on the one hand and the Critical or Controlling Parent on the other, to reflect the opposite ways in which parents behave towards their children.

As adults, the theory is, we harbour both Nurturing Parent and Critical Parent impressions and draw on them as we negotiate the various situations in life in which we need to nurture or control other people. There are obvious connections between this idea and the role of team leader. Susannah Temple (1990) developed a model of being in charge of others which contains the positive and negatives of Care and Control (Figure 6.2).

The model shows how the functions of parenting, care and control, can be positive or negative. When the balance between them is good, the effects on others is positive; when one or other is too great, the effects are likely to be negative.

When the *Care* function is experienced as *Nurturing* and the *Control* function as *Structuring*, people experience affirmation and are likely to develop high self-esteem. People usually feel good about themselves if they receive

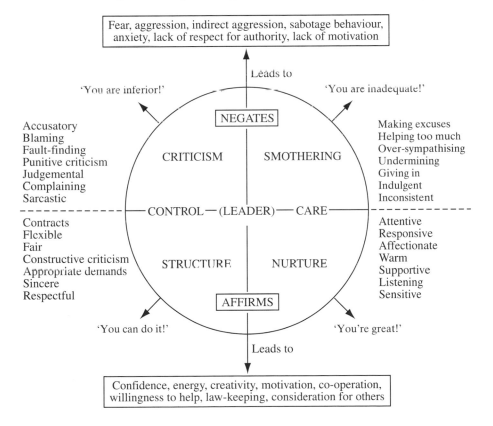

Figure 6.2: Leadership model using Parent ego state

consistent and reliable doses of inspiration and encouragement. When people feel good about themselves, they are more likely to succeed in what they do.

On the other hand, *Care* can be experienced as *Smothering* and *Control* as *Criticism*. These are the negative sides of control and care and link with different types of self-defeating behaviour.

Exercise 6.7: Being in Charge of Others

Group Structure: Whole group in role play.
Timing: 30 minutes.
Materials: Small cards each with a description of one of the functions of being in charge:

Card 1—*Criticism:* The main message to others is: 'You are inferior.' Your style is accusing, blaming, fault-finding, critical, punitive, judgemental, complaining, rigid, shouting, sarcastic.
Card 2—*Smothering:* The main message to others is: 'You are inadequate.' Your style is over-sympathetic, undermining, smothering, indulgent, interfering, inconsistent, too helpful, patronising.
Card 3—*Structuring:* The main message to others is: 'You can do it.' Your style is flexible, fair, definite, clear, open, consistent, sincere, kind, respectful, direct, commanding.
Card 4—*Nurturing:* The main message to others is: 'You're great!' Your style is attentive, accepting, responsive, gentle, sensitive, empathic, affectionate, understanding.

Process: Each person takes a card a random. You instruct people to act as far as possible in the style on the card in an activity which you set up or in a discussion.

After 10 minutes, ask people to take another card and continue, but in their new role.

Repeat this twice more—this means that everyone should have played each role.

After the role play, the discussion should focus on how people felt in the roles they played: Which did they feel most comfortable in? Least comfortable in? How did they find themselves responding to others? What does this tell them about appropriate leadership roles?

The next session focuses on one particular role which many people find themselves playing—attending or running a meeting. Meetings can be a source of frustration when they take a lot of time but apparently achieve little. This session offers some constructive and practical strategies for making meetings more effective.

SESSION 12: CONSTRUCTIVE MEETINGS

Training Objectives

1. To define necessary requirements for constructive meetings.
2. To explore ways of giving constructive feedback.
3. To explore formal and informal aspects of chairing a meeting.

Trainer Input

Let's take a few minutes to set the scene for this session:

Exercise 6.8: Best and Worst Meeting

Group Structure: Small group discussion or large group brainstorm.
Timing: 10 minutes.

Process: Ask people to remember the best meeting and the worst meeting they have ever attended and to list the things they feel contributed to making the meeting either good or bad.

Now that we have set the scene and identified what we need for a good meeting, let's consider how we can be most successful and influential in a meeting. Whenever people come together to work on a problem, issue or idea, three factors need to be considered if the outcome of the meeting is to be productive in terms of quality, acceptance and efficiency. These factors are:

- *Content:* What is to be worked on?
- *Methods:* Which systems, processes, structures and mechanisms will deal with the content?
- *People:* How do we treat ourselves and others during the meeting?

Often the content and method are more clearly defined and get more attention than people. Getting things done is a hallmark of a successful operation, but we all know how individuals or groups can sabotage successful functioning. People who are good at motivating and helping a group seem to be able to 'push' and 'pull' a group along. They push by stating clearly what they want, what they feel, what they think and applying rewards and pressure to encourage others. They pull by listening actively, exploring and building a common ground, raising hidden concerns and encouraging openness.

Exercise 6.9: Pushing and Pulling

Group Structure: Small working groups.
Timing: 30 minutes.
Materials: Worksheet for each participant.

Process: Hand out the worksheets which give examples of 'pushing' and 'pulling' behaviour for each of the three elements mentioned.

Ask each group to make up at least two more examples for each element. These can be compared and discussed by the whole group.

MEETINGS SKILLS WORKSHEET: PUSHING AND PULLING

	Push	*Pull*
CONTENT	I want to discuss the implication of this proposal for my area. I think the crucial factor here is the change in market share.	What do you believe will be the implications of this for the business? What do you think about this?
METHOD	I've got to leave by 3 o'clock. We should prioritise the agenda items.	Do you think 2 hours will be long enough for us to achieve what we need? How do you think we should tackle this?
PEOPLE	I'm getting irritated by the constant speech making. If you want our support you will need to contribute more to the meeting. Let's have a break to help us concentrate more.	You seem unhappy about what is happening. You seem angry; has something I've said upset you? It seems to me that we could do with a break to give us time to think.

A number of points are worth noting. The 'push' type of behaviour is very much concerned with self and with the person's own agenda, while the 'pull' type of behaviour is very much concerned with the other person and his or her agenda. It is not so much a question of which is 'good' or 'bad'—in fact each kind of initiative is important. To be most successful in groups a person needs to be able to 'push' and 'pull' when appropriate. Agendas can be open or hidden, so the more clearly articulated the agenda, the more likely the meeting is to be productive.

Many meetings require people to give and receive feedback. Feedback is a verbal or non-verbal process through which one person lets another know his or her perceptions, feelings and judgements about the other person's behaviour. It can, of course, be solicited or unsolicited. Unsolicited feedback can, at best, be surprising and, at worst, hurtful and is sometimes more likely to be fulfilling the needs of the giver than the receiver!

Exercise 6.10: Giving and Receiving Feedback

Group Structure: Pairs.
Timing: 10 minutes.

Process: Ask people to remember a time when they received feedback which helped them and a time when they received feedback which was hurtful, and to discuss the differences between these two occasions

---

In a meeting, feedback is most useful when it is consciously solicited either by the leader or chairperson or by individual members. For example, 'I'd value comments about the way I managed the meeting today—did you feel you had enough time to say what you wanted?' will encourage the members of the meeting to give you constructive feedback. To be constructive, feedback should focus on behaviour and not on the personality of the person or the intention behind it. Here are some 'golden rules':

- Take responsibility for what you communicate by using personal pronouns such as 'I' and 'my'. If you use terms like 'most people' or 'some members' it is difficult to know whether you really think and feel what you are saying or whether you are repeating the thoughts and feelings of others.
- Speak clearly and specifically, communicating your frame of reference, any assumptions you are making, your intention in communication or the leaps of thinking you are making. If you do this, people are more likely to understand your meaning rather than just hear the words.
- Make sure that your verbal and non-verbal languages are congruent with each other. Difficulties arise when your voice is saying one thing and your body another! Saying, 'I'm most interested in what you are saying' and yawning at the same time gives a very mixed message.
- Check that you have been correctly understood.

- Describe rather than evaluate or interpret. 'You keep interrupting me' is more helpful than 'You're a rotten, self-centred egoist who won't listen to anyone else's feelings!'
- Give feedback about things which can be changed.

Exercise 6.11: Feedback Practice

Group Structure: Small groups.
Timing: 20 minutes.

Process: Brief each small group to formulate a piece of feedback they could give to the other groups, according to the rules just discussed. When the groups come together, ask them to give the feedback to each other and discuss the reactions.

A successful meeting implies the arrival at useful solutions or decisions in which all members participate and feel able to express their own views and ideas. What are the skills which are most likely to make this happen?

Exercise 6.12: Meeting Skills Brainstorm

Timing: 5 minutes.

Process: Ask participants to call out skills which they think are necessary for good meetings and write them up on a flip chart. When they have finished you are likely to be able to put them into three categories: listening, supporting and constructive challenging.

Listening, supporting and challenging all make an important contribution to a successful meeting.

Let's consider *listening* first. When is it not happening? When people carry on more than one conversation at a time, interrupt each other and jump from one subject to another. When this happens vital information gets lost, ideas are not properly explored and decisions might be made too hastily. Effective listening is hard because people think more quickly than they speak, so it is tempting for us to develop our own thoughts while we are waiting for the slow arrival of the spoken word. This means that while someone else is talking you might be considering alternative arguments, evaluating what is being said, constructing difficult questions or, in fact, focusing on anything other than what the speaker is actually saying.

Exercise 6.13: The Cocktail Party

Group Structure: Pairs.
Timing: 2 minutes.

Process: When people are in pairs, sitting opposite each other, instruct them to tell each other their favourite childhood story at the same time! Tell them to keep talking for as long as they can at the same time as their partner.

When a couple of minutes have passed, stop them and ask for observations. People usually recount how difficult it is to keep talking once they have heard something the other person has said. The lesson is that we cannot listen and talk at the same time!

You can see how difficult it is to attend to what someone else is saying if you are talking. For communication to be successful the speaker and the listener each have responsibilities.
The speaker should:

- know exactly what she or he wants to say
- find appropriate words to express feelings and ideas
- actually speak these words.

The listener needs to:

- hear and understand the words
- check his or her understanding
- relate the communication to his or her own feelings and ideas and respond appropriately.

Exercise 6.14: Good Listening

Group Structure: Pairs.
Timing: 8 minutes.

Process: When participants are in pairs, brief them to take it in turns to talk about a matter of some importance to them. You can give them a subject if you wish. Explain that each will have his or her turn. One person will have 3 minutes in which to talk while the other listens and encourages that person to continue. When the 3 minutes are up, the listener is to repeat back what the speaker has said. The speaker can correct the listener, adding anything that has been missed or restating something that has been misunderstood. Repeat the process with the speaker and listener changing roles.

The feedback session should focus on those things people found easy or difficult, rewarding or stressful, etc.

Just as important as listening is the ability to be supportive. Some people, when presented with a new idea, seem to feel they must focus on its shortcomings. This can lead to a very negative atmosphere in which good ideas get missed, people become afraid to offer their thoughts and a climate of frustration and defensiveness develops. The overall effect in a meeting such as this is that people tend to protect and defend their own positions rather than work together as a team to produce an effective discussion. This negativity and lack of support contribute to a general ineffectiveness and lack of motivation in which goals tend to remain unmet.

When group members acknowledge and build on each other's ideas, the atmosphere feels much more supportive. Obviously not every idea which is presented is a good one, but even ideas which at first appear not to be useful often carry the seeds of something positive. So it is valuable to consider every suggestion as potentially valuable. To be supportive you need to:

- assume that other people's ideas are potentially useful
- listen carefully
- acknowledge any elements you find useful
- build on those
- appreciate the effort and energy that has gone into presenting the idea.

So we come to the third group of meeting skills—constructive challenging. It is possible for a meeting to have problems by being over-supportive, especially if people are worried about disrupting the feeling of togetherness by disagreeing with something.

However, it is possible to challenge in a constructive way. Listening and supporting are important here. If you can show that you have listened carefully to and recognised the merits in someone else's argument, then that person is more likely to be willing to accept and consider areas of disagreement. When challenging or disagreeing, it is important to use language which suggests concern about the idea rather than describing how wrong the person is. 'What concerns me most about this is . . . ' is better than

'You can't be serious!'; 'The problem I see in this is . . . ' is better than 'You are wrong to suggest . . . '.

Notes for the Trainer

You could develop this session by introducing role plays of meetings or skills exercises. Depending on the particular interests of the group you might want to focus on preparation, agenda setting, time management, note taking, assertion, dealing with difficult people, leading or chairing a meeting and so on. It is useful to finish such a session by introducing the idea of evaluating each meeting for effectiveness.

Trainer Input

So far we have concentrated on the kind of behaviour that is most likely to help a meeting to a constructive conclusion, but let us now take a look at how things can go wrong. Resistance of different kinds can happen at a meeting, particularly when group members feel no ownership or responsibility for the meeting. In this situation, people are willing for responsibility to lie with the leader or chair who is supposed to control what goes on. It is useful to recognise that very often resistance is a reaction to an emotional process taking place within the 'resister' rather than an authentic response to the issue at hand. It can be a reaction to the fear of change or a way to counteract unwanted control. Whatever the reason, it can take different forms.

- *Blocking:* This occurs when someone goes off at a tangent, focusing on irrelevant details or over-arguing a particular point. The overall effect is to divert attention from the issue to the 'blocker'.
- *Power seeking:* This tends to occur in groups with hierarchical structures. Individuals or cliques get involved in conflict with the leader, which results in a power struggle of some sort. The result is a split group with people taking sides and, once again, attention is drawn away from the issue.
- *Attention seeking:* This happens when someone talks, often in an intellectualising style, at length. He or she might advocate extreme ideas or behave unusually. The attention seeking might take the form of making self-centred comments or recounting irrelevant anecdotes, thus drawing attention to the speaker.
- *Dominating:* This can be recognised in individuals or small groups who speak loudly, make speeches rather than discuss and lobby for their own issues. What happens is that this has the effect of silencing the less forceful members who then begin to feel controlled and resentful.
- *Clowning:* This is a type of behaviour which can have a positive or a

negative effect. When appropriate it can lighten the mood and dispel tension; but if persistent the clown can disrupt the meeting's progress.

- *Silence:* This can indicate passive aggression demonstrated by a person who may well be very hostile to what is being said but unable or unwilling to express his or her feelings directly.
- *Compliance:* This, like silence, can be taken as agreement by someone who is using compliance to resist agreement with the leader or chair. While this person will appear to be in agreement—if in a somewhat lukewarm manner—it is possible he or she may well reveal reservations or disagreement at a future meeting—after agreement seems to have been reached.

Exercise 6.15: Role-Play Meeting

Group Structure: Groups of up to 8.
Timing: 1 hour.
Materials: Briefing cards for each person. If there is more than one group, separate rooms are desirable.

Process: Tell the group that they will be holding a meeting and that each person will be given a brief as to how to behave. They are to imagine they are planning to paint a room and need to agree on a colour. Give out the briefs and allow the meeting to proceed for about 20 minutes. Then hold a feedback session where people can talk about their reactions to what happened and compare these with other meetings they have attended.

The briefs, which should be written on separate cards, are as follows:

1. You are the leader of the meeting; you have no preference as to the colour. It is more important to you that the decision is an agreed one.
2. You don't really care what colour is chosen, but you feel very strongly that the floor covering should be washable and the curtains colourful.
3. You want the room to be painted red—no other colour will do for you.
4. You want the room to be painted blue—no other colour will do for you.
5. You don't mind what colour the room is, but you want to be on the 'winning side'.
6. You don't like the idea of changing the colour at all but don't want to start an argument in case you end up feeling 'out on a limb'.
7. You think the whole thing is a bit of a joke; not worth arguing about.
8. You want any colour other than red or blue.

Notes for the Trainer

This particular exercise can be adapted to match your situation. You can write the briefs to include any particular form of resistance you wish, and you can run the exercise with fewer or more people. The point is to give participants some experience of facing the kind of resistance which often occurs during a meeting and then to analyse what happened.

You might decide to end with a discussion as to the wisest ways of dealing with these problems. Here are some guidelines:

- Identify for yourself the form the resistance is taking, express your thoughts and confront it in an atmosphere of care and concern rather than punishment.
- Focus on the behaviour itself rather than the individual.
- Point out the effects of resistance; it may be the case that the person does not actually realise how his or her behaviour is affecting others.
- Suggest alternative forms of behaviour that will result in more satisfying participation for both the 'resister' and everyone else.

This chapter has explored some of the issues which are raised by the various roles and responsibilities people may have in their organisation. Our next chapter focuses on what happens when things go wrong.

REFERENCES

Adair, J. (1987). *Effective Teambuilding*. Gower Publishing.
Belbin, R.M. (1981). *Management Teams; Why They Succeed or Fail*. Heinemann.
Egan, G. (1982). *The Skilled Helper*. California: Brooks/Cole.
Hardingham, A. (1995). *Working in Teams*. Institute of Personnel and Development.
Temple, S. (1990). Who's in charge, a model for behaviour management. *ITA News*, No. 27.

7

CONFLICTS AND CLASHES

One of the more unpleasant aspects working in an organisation is having to deal with conflict. In this chapter we will look at different ways of helping people to manage such situations as constructively as possible.

SESSION 13: UNDERSTANDING CONFLICT

TRAINING OBJECTIVES

1. To identify sources and forms of conflict
2. To clarify and discuss the effects on individuals and the organisation.
3. To consider different perspectives on conflict

Notes for the Trainer

One way in which organisations try to solve the problems caused by conflicts between staff which are interfering with the efficient meeting of objectives is to call in a trainer. Conflict can spring from a number of sources, and to design effective training structures, the trainer needs to be as clear as possible as to the root of the problems. Effective training needs analysis is particularly important for this kind of training. Conflict, for instance, can arise through misunderstandings due to poor communication, structural elements such as size or the way in which individuals are actually behaving. The extent to which one, some or all of these factors might be causing the problem will influence the type of training you may decide to offer. The danger of not having enough information is that your training may not be targeted well enough and may make things worse rather than better.

Another important influence on your design decisions will be whether you are being asked to train managers to deal with clashes they may have to resolve, front-line staff who have to cope with confrontations from members of the public, or workers who are actually themselves in conflict with each other.

Working with people who are not getting on together has obvious potential tensions and requires a great deal of sensitivity. One way of approaching this work is to offer a rather theoretical and general introduction, encouraging group members to draw out insights about their particular situation. This session can act as such an introduction.

Trainer Input

During this training session we are exploring ideas about conflict, where it comes from, why it happens, different ways of perceiving it and how it affects us. This exploration will help us move on to decide on the best ways of handling or resolving conflicts which we may face either now or in the future.

Firstly, what actually is it? Here are a couple of definitions.

- *Conflict involves incompatible differences between parties that result in interference or opposition.* (Vecchio, 1995)
- *Conflict is a state of mind. It has to be perceived by the parties involved. If two or more parties are not aware of a conflict, then no conflict exists.* (Huczynski & Buchanan, 1991)
- *Conflict is the process which results when one person (or a group of people) perceives that another person or group is frustrating, or is about to frustrate, an important concern.* (Thomas, 1976)

Exercise 7.1: What's Going On

Group Structure: Threes or fours for short discussion.
Timing: 10 minutes.

Process: Ask people to recall a conflict in which they have been involved. Tell them that they will be able to use this example from time to time during this session to demonstrate some of the ideas. Suggest that, meantime, they tell each other about the conflict—the people involved, how it started, ways in which they are affected and so on. Referring to the definitions you gave, ask them to check how they relate to their examples.

There are various possible sources of conflict but most of them fall into one of three categories.

Firstly, conflict can arise from bad communication. A simple definition of communication is the ability to understand and be understood. It is probably a rarity that someone understands someone else perfectly. Faulty communication can result in information being understood incorrectly, distortedly or ambiguously. In turn this can create a great deal of hostility.

Then there are certain structural factors which affect the quality of relationships in an organisation. Size, for instance, is important. Very often success leads to an increase in the size of an organisation which in turn can lead to less clarity about goals, less informal contact between individuals or departments and more possibilities of information becoming distorted because it passes through more levels. The differences which exist among staff members can cause problems; for instance, there may be conflict between different levels of authority, length of service or preferred patterns of working. Conflict can also arise out of differences in the level of participation of staff in decision making; whether or not reward systems exist and whether they are seen to be fair; competition for resources; the patterns of power distribution and so on.

There is a third possible source of conflict and that lies in possible differences of values, perceptions or behaviour between individuals. As a result of their perceptions, people can come to speedy assessments of each other's behaviour. If the perception is faulty—conflict is likely to ensue.

Exercise 7.2: Communication Clashes

Group Structure: Whole group brainstorm.
Timing: Up to 5 minutes.
Materials: Flip chart and pen.

Process: Ask the group to call out any examples of typical situations which might lead to conflict. When the group run out of items give them a little time to decide which of the three categories you have talked about is likely to have initiated the problem. If there are any problems which do not fit into these categories, invite the group to widen the list.

Having identified some possible and predictable sources of conflict let us now look at the different forms that conflict can take. There are two main distinctions—collective or intergroup conflict, which involves large numbers of people acting together, and individual conflict, which is intrapersonal in nature with far less people, perhaps only two, involved.

Martin Jelfs (1982) points out that studies of group dynamics have shown similarities in the kind of problems which emerge in groups. These can be summed up as:

- *Problems of dominance and leadership:* There are a variety of reasons as to why people become dominant in a group. They may have most information or feel most strongly about the task; they may have a naturally extrovert personality; they may feel insecure unless they feel in control and so on.

- *Elitism:* There are also many reasons why a particular group may come to have power over others. They might be a friendship clique with very strong ties; they may be seen as more valuable because of their knowledge or experience.
- *Boredom:* People can get bored if they experience their work as un-interesting, repetitive, unrewarding, over-taxing. The boredom can lead to feelings of alienation which, in turn, can lead to a certain lack of care or actual destructiveness as tasks are carried out. Conflict is likely to ensue.
- *Confusion:* This can arise because people have too much to do in too short a time; because they react to what is happening at different rates; because they do not have the necessary understanding of the history, facts or implications of the present situation. Jargon can be confusing to those not familiar with it; organisations often develop habitual ways of doing things which again can confuse anyone not initiated into the ritual. Goals can potentially be in conflict with each other—for example, goals to provide a comprehensive service and to see as many clients as possible have obvious possible problems.
- *Hidden agendas:* These are often a cause of conflict because if an individual, or a small group, is covertly trying to control others towards particular actions or decisions, people are going to feel manipulated or dissatisfied.
- *Broken agreements:* These have a very destructive effect. People arriving late for meetings, not delivering services or goods as promised, not finishing tasks according to agreed deadlines or standards of quality and so on are all possible conflict points.

The presence of these kinds of conflict points can create an unpleasantly distrustful atmosphere in which people's motives are constantly questioned and the most negative interpretation placed on actions.

Exercise 7.3: Points of Conflict

Group Structure: Small discussion groups as in the last exercise.
Timing: 10 minutes.

Process: Ask the group to refer to the various conflicts they identified to find out whether they can relate these suggestions as to the sources of conflict in their actual situations. Once again, if they identify any other sources, these can be discussed during the feedback session.

Notes for the Trainer

At this point you could continue the exploration of conflicts which may be affecting your training group. Whether you choose to do this depends on the brief you have been given by the organisation. If you do decide to continue looking at group dynamics, here are some exercises which will help you.

Exercise 7.4: Them and Us

Group Structure: Whole group split into two or three 'factions'.
Timing: Up to 60 minutes.
Materials: Two or three sheets of flip-chart paper for each group, felt-tip pens, blu-tack or drawing pins. You will need separate rooms for groups.

Process: This exercise is most effective when the group is actually split into two or three factions. It works best when each group can work in a different room; they need to be well out of earshot of each other. Each group is asked to create a three-dimensional image of the other group(s), starting by answering the three questions:

- How do we see Us in relation to Them?
- How do we think They see Us?
- How do We see Them?

Groups should aim for a consensus before they write their answers on the wall charts. When they have answered the questions in words, they should create an image which they feel represents the other group(s) in some way.

When the groups come together, the wall charts should be displayed. The ensuing discussion should be directed towards a greater under-standing of each group's perception of the other, focusing on the accuracy or otherwise of the images.

Exercise 7.5: Shared Assessment

Group Structure: Similar to Exercise 7.4, splitting into opposing groups.
Timing: 60–90 minutes.
Materials: Sheets of flip-chart paper; pens; drawing pins.

Process: Give each group 15 minutes to assess the other by brainstorming lists of:

- Positive aspects
- Negative aspects
- Constructive suggestions for change

Next, ask them to do the same thing for themselves. Each group ends up with six lists. Groups then exchange their assessments of each other so that both groups now have two evaluations on themselves. Staying in their two groups, they discuss the lists, paying particular attention to the constructive suggestions.

When the two groups come together, ask each person to pair up with someone from the other group to discuss their thoughts and feelings about the exercise. Each pair can then meet with another pair and so on until the group is working together as a whole.

Notes for the Trainer

Each of these exercises require a certain measure of disclosure from individuals about their thoughts and feelings with regard to themselves and others. The exercises are based on the fact that many group conflicts are caused by blockages in communication. They aim to create a situation in which people feel secure enough to share their perceptions honestly and constructively. You may find yourself needing to act as a mediator between the groups during feedback sessions. If the conflict is too deep to be resolved in this way, there is the option of involving a mediator from outside the organisation.

The exercises need to be chosen with care; there is always the danger that the group will become more polarised as a result of the work.

The next part of this session focuses on different perceptions of conflict.

Trainer Input

The main point of exploring conflict is to help us decide on the best way of resolving the problems it may bring. There is one more important element of this exploration before we move onto more practical matters and that is the different ways in which conflict can be perceived.

Traditional Perspective

This is the view that conflict represents a malfunction within a group, department, or organisation and should therefore be avoided at all costs. Graeme Salaman (1981) described how organisations tended to be presented from this perspective:

- harmonious, co-operative structures
- no systematic conflicts of interest arising
- conflicts that do arise seen as exceptional
- conflicts are assumed to originate from misunderstandings
- confusions, personality factors, extra-organisational factors outside the organisation's control and the expectations from stubborn and inflexible employees.

Salaman points out that to maintain this idea of the ideal conflict-free organisation, conflicts have to be explained away. The easiest way to do this is to point to mismanagement, bad communication or unco-operative employees.

Behavioural Perspective
This is the view which sees conflict as a natural, inevitable phenomenon to be found in all organisations. In this perspective, conflict is seen as actually reinforcing the status quo. Within limits, conflict is believed to help change through evolution rather than revolution. It acts as a safety valve and keeps organisations responsive to internal and external changes while retaining their own essential elements like the hierarchy and power distribution. Conflict arises out of the way individuals and groups pursue their own objectives. Managing effectively in this situation means being able to come to decisions which contain the differences usually by effecting compromise to encourage collaboration.

Interactionist Perspective
This perspective goes further than just managing conflict. It sees conflict as something to encourage. The argument is that groups which are peaceful, harmonious and co-operative can become lacking in vitality and unresponsive to changing needs. Rather than trying to eliminate conflict, managers according to this perspective should create just the right level of conflict in order to gain its benefits. These benefits could well include:

- Helping to bring about change by challenging the status quo.
- Increasing group cohesiveness by creating an 'external threat'—a well-known method of getting people to forget their differences and pull together.
- Creating more trust, openness and support through successful conflict resolution.

Radical Perspective
Taking things even further, this is essentially a Marxist perspective which sees lack of conflict as the problem. The Marxist view sees conflict as a way of bringing about revolutionary change. The argument is that there is a disparity of power between the owners and controllers ('the bosses') of economic resources and those who depend on access to these resources for their living ('the workers').

Graeme Salaman (1981) describes organisations as arenas for individual and group conflict. The fight can be for scarce resources, individual career advancement, 'perks', and so on. Organisational goals are used to justify or to legitimate rather than to determine behaviour. The belief on which this perspective exists is that individual and organisational interests will rarely coincide. Salaman describes how the political dimension of organisational employment is revealed in the unequal nature of organisational life and the constant possibility of subordinates resisting or avoiding the efforts of their seniors to control them. He makes the point that workers who experience inferior work conditions, which result in insecurity, deprivation, dehumanised work and subordination, are likely to demonstrate resistance to the oppression to which they are subject.

Exercise 7.6: Perspectives on Conflict (1)

Group Structure: Work in pairs leading to group discussion.
Timing: 30–50 minutes.
Materials: Perspectives worksheet for each person.

PERSPECTIVES ON CONFLICT WORKSHEET
Conflict can take many forms. Here are some examples taken from Taylor and Walton's contribution to *Images of Deviance*, published by Penguin Books in 1971:

1. A worker in a sweet factory demonstrated his frustration by ensuring that the message 'Fuck Off' ran through half a mile of Blackpool Rock. He was dismissed.
2. Railwaymen described how they block lines with trucks to delay shunting operations for a few hours.
3. In factories material is hidden, conveyor belts jammed with sticks, cogs stopped with wire ropes, lorries 'accidentally' backed into ditches.
4. Electricians put in weak fuses; textile workers 'knife' through carpets ; farm workers co-operate to choke agricultural machinery with tree branches.
5. Computing facilities have to be defended against deliberate sabotage with computer viruses.

Taking these examples as your starting point review how each might be explained by someone taking a

- Traditional perspective
- Behaviourist perspective
- Interactionist perspective
- Radical perspective

Take an example of conflict from your own experience and try to explain it from each of the above perspective.s

Process: Suggest that people take a few minutes to read through the worksheet and then, in pairs, discuss their thoughts. Bring the pairs together and continue the discussion in the large group.

Notes for the Trainer

The aim of this part of the session is to demonstrate that people working in organisations can have very different views of the organisation and their place in it. It is not so much a question of deciding which is the 'best' or 'right' view but of understanding the nature and implications of the differences. For instance, in a dispute between management and workers, if management argue from the traditional perspective with workers who are perceiving the situation from the radical perspective, it is not difficult to see how the conflict will not easily be resolved.

Exercise 7.7: Perspectives on Conflict (2)

Group Structure: Small workshop groups reporting back to large group.
Timing: 30 minutes.
Materials: A set of newspapers reporting a current industrial dispute for each group.

Process: Using the newspapers provided (as many different ones as possible) each group is to identify the views of management, workers, unions and journalists as either traditional, behaviourist, interactionist or radical. Interesting points to note are how different perspectives may be helping or hindering successful resolution of the conflict; how different perspectives influence reporting; and so on.

SESSION 14: RESOLVING CONFLICT

Training Objectives

1. To present a conflict analysis checklist
2. To introduce five conflict resolution management styles.

3. To consider the appropriateness of each style.
4. To practise conflict resolution skills

Trainer Input

In this session we are looking at practical ways of managing conflict. Firstly, here is a checklist which will help you to clarify the nature of the conflict you want to manage. Checklists are very useful. They act as reminders at times of stress and can guide our management of a situation.

Exercise 7.8: Questions about Conflicts

Group Structure: Individual work, followed by group discussion.
Timing: 15–20 minutes.
Materials: Copy of checklist for each person.

Process: Ask participants to identify a conflict in which they are engaged at present (or if there isn't one, to remember one from the past). The group discussion following this can focus on insights which people may get through completing the checklist, any useful questions they feel could be added, and thoughts as to what appear to be the main problems.

CONFLICT CHECKLIST

Below is a selection of questions you could ask yourself to help you decide which conflict management stance to take. When you have completed the questionnaire as far as you can, take time to consider the situation again. The checklist is in four sections and contains questions about yourself, about the others involved, about other people who are not directly involved and about the organisation.

Self (as the person responsible for managing the situation)

- What can I do?
- What do I want the outcome to be?
- What are my responsibilities?
- Can I manage this conflict fairly?
- Are there any particular areas of discomfort for me regarding the people and issues involved?
- Are there any aspects of this conflict that I would prefer not to deal with? If so, what can I do about them?
- What personal strengths can I draw on to help me?

- What personal weaknesses might stand in the way?
- Do I have the necessary knowledge to deal with this?
- Do I have the necessary skills?
- Do I have the necessary authority/status to act effectively?
- What is the quality of my relationship with the people involved? Is it likely to be affected? If so, how?
- Do I have the time to deal with this effectively?
- Add your own questions: . . .

Other Parties Involved in the Conflict

- Who are they? What do I know about them?
- What is the outcome they are probably hoping for?
- Have they been in similar situations before?
- How do they normally behave?
- Are there any aspects of their personality which might make it difficult to work with them?
- Are there any particular personal strengths they have which might help?
- Are there any particular personal weaknesses which might stand in the way?
- How aware are the other parties of the effect of their behaviour/ attitude?
- Do they have the knowledge they need about the situation?
- Have they acted competently? How much is the issue at stake to do with lack of competence?
- How much is the problem linked to inequality in levels of power, authority and status?
- What are the implications of not resolving the conflict?
- Add your own questions: . . .

Others Not Directly Involved

- Who else is affected by the conflict?
- How does it affect them?
- Will it be necessary to involve them in the conflict resolution process?
- Are their views important? If so, how can they be considered?
- Add your own questions: . . .

Organisation

- Are there any organisational or legal rules which should guide the resolution process? If so, what are they?
- Are there any existing procedures and structures in the organisation? If so, are they appropriate for this situation?

- What resources are available? What are the limits to resources?
- What time factors or deadlines are operating?
- How does the culture of the organisation affect the situation?
- Add your own questions: . . .

This type of checklist will help you clarify the situation and point you towards your possible options for action. You might decide that ranking will help you further. This will give you an impression of priorities and is essential when safety is an issue. Ask yourself:

- What is the most important feature of the situation?
- Who is the most powerful person involved?
- Who is most at risk?
- What is the next most important feature?

You can go on asking yourself this series of questions until you have ranked all the elements.

Strategies for Handling Conflict
K.W. Thomas (1976) has suggested five major styles of conflict management: competitive, collaborative, accommodating, compromising and avoiding.

Competitive
This could be best summed up with the phrase 'Might is right'. It is the typical style of someone who is highly assertive with regard to his or her own interests. This party will experience the situation as a battle which has to be won. The other side is 'the enemy', to be overcome through formal authority, threats or the use of power.

Collaborative
'We'll do it together' describes this style. Here both parties work to satisfy their concerns though adopting a problem-solving approach. The people involved trust each other and are willing to work together to get the best possible resolution for each of them.

Accommodating
'We'll do it your way' is the motto here. Here one party puts the other party's interests first. It can be seen as either giving in or a demonstration of altruism.

Compromising
'Fifty-fifty' sums up this approach. Each party is willing to give up something so that agreement can be reached. No one loses everything and no one wins everything—but everyone gets something.

Avoiding
'There's no problem' is the complete discounting of the seriousness of the situation. Here one or both of the parties involved may recognise there is a conflict but chooses to ignore it in the hope it will go away. Conflicts very rarely go away of their own accord; sometimes the conflict appears to have receded but crops up in another form. In situations where people who have differences which cannot be resolved have to work together, they are required to suppress the conflict. Managers may adopt this avoiding style at the outset of a conflict, leaving time for the people involved to resolve it themselves and only intervening if a solution does not appear to arise.

Exercise 7.9: Resolving Conflicts

Group Structure: Seminar groups.
Timing: 30 minutes in seminar group plus large group discussion.

Process: Ask participants to think of at least three different conflict situations in which they have been involved either at work or at home. Give them time to note down the essential details of each one and then ask them to answer the following questions. Their answers can be discussed in the seminar group and general learning points drawn out in a plenary session.

- Of the five styles we have discussed (competing, collaborating, accommodating, compromise and avoiding) which is nearest the style you adopted in each of the situations you have chosen?
- Which style did your opponent adopt?
- Looking over each of your situations, would you say that you have a single conflict management style or do you use different styles for different occasions?

Here is a guide to general agreements as to when each of these styles would be most useful:

Competition
- In an emergency when decisive action is vital.
- When important but unpopular actions need implementing.
- When the issue is vital to individual or organisational welfare.
- When you are opposing someone who takes advantage of non-competitive behaviour.

Collaborating

- When both sides are representing issues too important to compromise.
- When you want to learn from the other side.
- When you want to help people with different views work together.
- When you want people to feel committed to decision or action.

Accommodating

- When you are in the wrong.
- When the matters of concern are more important to others than yourself.
- To lessen the loss when you are on the losing side.
- When the most important outcome is harmony and co-operation.

Compromise

- To achieve temporary agreements in complex issues.
- To speed up resolution when time is pressing.
- When each side is equally powerful.
- To fall back on when competition or collaboration is unsuccessful.

Avoidance

- When the issue is unimportant or low in order of priority.
- When confronting the conflict will cause more disruption than advantage.
- To give people time to cool down.
- When time to think or gather information is more important than an immediate outcome.
- When someone else is more likely to resolve matters.

Notes for the Trainer

How you continue this training depends on the particular brief you have been given. What follows is a description of two examples of training interventions. They are all based on the assumption that your objectives are to help course participants to understand and deal with conflicts they are experiencing. In order for these training sessions to be successful you will need to establish a certain amount of positive motivation from all those taking part. Sometimes people are so tired of the situation they just do not feel like doing anything about it.

This kind of intervention serves two purposes—one is obviously to help resolve the conflict; the other is to provide a model for individuals or groups to use if conflicts arise in the future. You may, for instance, use the first example, a structure to help two people resolve a conflict, as a teaching demonstration.

Example 1: Interpersonal Conflict

This is probably the simplest type of conflict—where two people are engaged in a conflict which they are not able to resolve by themselves. Times are not given because the process depends very much on working at the participants' pace and giving time for everything that needs to be said.

Stage 1: Briefly go over the history and intention of the meeting. Possible goals might be to restore some degree of co-operation; to understand the root of the trouble; to decide what practical steps could be taken to prevent a similar occurrence in the future.

Stage 2. Describe the 'ground rules' for the session:

- Take it in turns to talk
- No interrupting
- Reflect back what the other person is saying before making a new point.

Stage 3: Invite one person to tell the other specifically what behaviour it is that irritates or displeases. It is important that the person ONLY talks about behaviour and does not make personal statements such as, 'You are so slovenly/picky/unpunctual . . . '.

Stage 4: Ask the other person to repeat, in his or her own words, what the first person has said. Ask questions like:

- 'Do you understand what he/she is getting at?'
- 'Can you put it into your own words?'
- 'Do you know how this started?'

   If the person is finding it difficult to understand, continue to try to clarify things:

- 'Try describing it again'
- 'Is there something which irritates you most?'
- 'What would you like him/her to do now?'

Stage 5: Give the other person the same opportunity, keeping to the same guidelines. If you notice either person becoming defensive or aggressive, encourage him or her to stay with describing behaviour in specific terms. From time to time, summarise what is being said and check that your summary is acceptable to both parties.

   At this point, the situation may be resolved—sometimes the problem is that one or other of the people involved just have not realised the effect of their behaviour. In many cases, they are perfectly willing to modify or change what they are doing.

Stage 6: If it isn't enough, however, you can encourage the people to brainstorm possible actions. Questions like:

- 'What could be done about this?'
- 'Is there anything which could reduce the amount of tension between you?'
- 'What are you willing to change?'

Stage 7: Once again, this may be enough to resolve things. If not, people may have to settle for living with their differences and tolerate a certain amount of tension. Even if this is the best outcome, the air will have been cleared and communication will be more direct.

Make sure that you set down any agreement reached in clear and concrete terms. Any agreement should contain decisions about how long a trial period the parties want as well as the actual changes that are agreed. Stating what criteria will be used to assess whether the agreement is working is also useful.

Notes for the Trainer

The next example focuses on team conflict and assumes that the team in which there is a problem is present at the training session and that they have contracted to work on their problem. A key element in the session is time given to enable people to exchange information about themselves, their jobs, their aims and their perceptions.

Problems often occur in a team because people get so wrapped up in their own particular tasks that they lose sight of the needs of the others.

Example 2: Conflicts in Teams

Stage 1: Give each participant time to write down on a sheet of flip-chart paper a short description of his or her own job; the three most important priorities for the next year; and which activities from other members of the team would help. When the wall sheets are displayed, there should be a discussion of each one focusing on whether the expectations of each other are clear. (30 minutes.)

Stage 2: Give each person sheets of paper on which they can write the names of every other person in the team. (A different sheet for each person.) Ask each person to write down brief notes on what behaviour in team members hinders or helps him or her most. When finished, each person collects the sheets of paper that contain his or her name. Each participant then gives a summary of the perception they received from the notes as well as any questions they need to ask. (At least 2 hours.)

Stage 3: Give participants time to decide what they are willing to do to contribute to reducing the conflict between team members. Each person then gives a summary of his or her intentions; these are converted into contracts which are written down.

As in the previous example, a review session needs to be written in so that people can decide whether they need to modify or change their decisions.

SESSION 15: NEGOTIATION

Training Objectives

1. To introduce the concept of principled negotiation.
2. To identify skills necessary for principled negotiation.
3. To practise skills.
4. To consider strategies if an agreement cannot be reached.

Notes for the Trainer

Negotiation skills are very relevant to this exploration of the understanding and management of problems which can arise as a result of breakdown in communication. The next session offers a structure to the introduction of a particular style of negotiation which can be adapted for use in a variety of situations from one-to-one relationships in which the communication has broken down to the large scene of industrial disputes between management and workers.

When presenting the input, which is quite long, you could choose to slot in short 'buzz group' sessions, asking participants to work in pairs or small groups sharing their own ideas and experiences relating to each of the four principles.

Trainer Input

Very often a conflict situation can only be resolved through some kind of formal negotiation. Standard strategies for negotiation often require the negotiator to decide on a hard or a soft position. The hard negotiator sees each situation as a battle of wills which he or she wants to win—at all costs. The soft negotiator wants to avoid personal conflict and so makes concessions in order to avoid conflict and reach an agreement. Roger Fisher and William Ury (1982) offer an alternative to the usual 'hard' and 'soft' styles of negotiating which they call Principled Negotiation and it is upon this style that we will now focus.

There are four main elements to this kind of negotiating:

Separate the People from the Problem

When people negotiate from a 'hard' or 'soft' position, inevitably their own egos become identified with 'winning' or 'losing'. This makes it difficult for them to work impartially for the wisest resolution, because if they are negotiating on something that is important to them, their emotions will probably become entangled with the objective merits of the problem. Fisher and Ury suggest that, before working on the actual content of the problem, you disentangle any 'people problems' which you feel are present. The aim is that the participants should come to see themselves as working co-operatively rather than competitively and to tackle the problem rather than each other. People problems, if they exists, should be tackled first—and separately from the negotiation.

Some guidelines to doing this are:

- Put yourself in the other person's shoes to attempt to understand his or her point of view as accurately as possible.
- Don't assume that he or she is actually intending what you fear.
- Don't blame him or her for your problem.
- Be willing to talk to each other about your perceptions.
- Look for opportunities to make positive contact.
- Recognise and understand the emotions that are being experienced by you and the other person.
- Talk about these feelings, acknowledging them as legitimate.
- Allow the other person to let off steam if necessary, but don't react to these outbursts of emotion as if they were personal attacks.
- Use your active listening skills and acknowledge what is being said.

Put your Main Focus on Interests rather than Positions

The point of this is to overcome the drawback of focusing on the stated positions when the object of a negotiation is to satisfy underlying interests. A negotiating position often covers up what you really want. Compromising between positions is not likely to produce an agreement which will take care of the human needs which led to the adoption of the positions. Rather than continue to press your position, take some time to acknowledge whatever common interests there may be.

- Remember that it is interests which define the problem.
- Behind opposed positions lie shared and compatible interests as well as conflicting ones.
- *Different* interests are not necessarily the same as *conflicting* interests.
- Ask 'why?' and 'why not?' to help you identify interests.
- Remember Maslow—the most powerful interests are basic human needs.

Invent Options for Mutual Gain

It is difficult to design optimal solutions while under pressure. Trying to make a decision in the presence of an 'enemy' restricts your vision. Set aside a designated time within which to think up a wide range of possible solutions which advance shared interests and reconcile differing interests. Four major obstacles that inhibit the inventing of an abundance of options are:

- Making judgements too quickly.
- Believing that there is only one answer.
- The assumption that circumstances surrounding the negotiation are unable to change and that resources are fixed.
- The attitude that it is *their* responsibility to solve *their* problem.

Bearing this in mind, when you are inventing options:

- Separate *inventing* from *deciding*.
- Seek to broaden the options rather than search for a single answer.
- Try as hard as possible to find options which will provide mutual gains.
- Invent ways of making it easy for the other side to decide.

Insist on Objective Criteria to Evaluate the Decision
However much you have understood the interests of the other side, and however well you have invented ways of reconciling the different interests, there may well remain some interests that are still in conflict. In this case, unless you resort to trying to win by being stubborn, you need to find a way of evaluating an agreement which each side will accept as just. This means referring to standards of fairness, efficiency or scientific merit. The more it is possible to relate to precedent and past organisational or community practice, the more likely you are to reach a proposal which is fair and wise.
    Here are some guidelines:

- Seek for fair standards so that the final agreement could be based upon

market value	precedent
scientific judgement	equal rights
moral standards	the law
tradition	efficiency
cost	professional codes
and so on.	

- Present the issue as a joint search for objective criteria (e.g. 'Let's start by discussing what a fair price might be').
- Keep an open mind and be willing to listen to the other side's reasons for the proposals

Notes for the Trainer

This is the end of the input to present the basic ideas behind Fisher and Ury's Principled Negotiation. The practical work with which you decide to follow this depends on the purpose of the training and on the time you have available. If you are introducing a group of trainee managers to these principles you will probably design a role play based on fictional characters in which people take on the various roles and play out the negotiation. Here is an example of a very simple role play in which pairs work together, each having been given a particular brief. The character briefs can be created to match situations that trainees are likely to meet.

Exercise 7.10: Negotiation Skills

Group Structure: Role play in pairs; debriefing and discussion by large group.
Timing: At least an hour.
Materials: Briefing sheets for each participant. The briefs will be in sets of two with a separate sheet for each partner.

Process: Give out the briefing sheets, and suggest that people take 10–15 minutes to prepare. The actual role play can be audio or video taped so that people can refer back to what happened; or the exercise can be set up in groups of three—with one person acting as an observer.

EXAMPLES OF BRIEFING SHEETS.

Brief 1: The Advice Bureau
You are the manager of an advice/counselling service, responsible for a team of four full-time paid staff.

Your bureau is in an urban area with many problems of homelessness, redundancy, debt, etc., so your service is very hard pressed. Your bureau is part of a national network and head office is making demands on you to increase the number of clients seen as well as insisting on a high standard of work.

One member of your staff is giving you cause for concern. This person, who has been very reliable until now, has become unpunctual, often coming in late. The quality of case-recording has deteriorated and is actually rather sloppy. This worker's mind always seems to be somewhere else and one or two clients have asked to see someone else, even though it means a longer wait for them.

You know that there have been some changes in this person's family life—there is a new baby—but you've been too busy to engage in conversation to find out how things are.

You have asked this worker to meet with you as you feel you can no longer ignore the effect on other workers, who are beginning to grumble.

Prepare for the meeting.

Brief 2: Advice Worker/Counsellor
You are an advice worker/counsellor in a small team that is part of a larger organisation. For some time you have been unhappy about the standard of work that the team has been achieving. You believe the reason is poor management by the team leader.

You have recently become a parent and are taking some time to adjust to this new situation. You expected your fellow workers to be sympathetic to your difficulties during this period of adjustment.

Now you are confronted by the manager complaining about your time keeping and the standard of your work—e.g. case recording not being up to scratch.

You have been feeling more and more aggrieved about the fact that the manager never bothers to socialise with staff. You feel that you are getting more than your fair share of the difficult cases but are not getting the support that you need at this time. You also feel that you are being made the scapegoat for the team's problems. You know, for instance, that a lot of pressure is being put on the service by head office who are demanding higher standards.

The manager has arranged to meet with you.

Prepare for the meeting.

Trainer Input

The strategies we have explored are most likely to lead you to some resolution of the difficulties, but they are not magic. It would be useful, therefore, to consider what options are available to us if the negotiation is not working. Firstly, Fisher and Ury (1982) suggest that you think about the 'Best Alternative To a Negotiated Agreement' (your BATNA).

Considering interest, options and standards is not much use when the other side is in a much stronger bargaining position through being richer, better connected, or having more power. No method guarantees success if all the leverage is on the other side.

Rather than thinking out your 'bottom line', which tends to be based on the worst acceptable outcome, concentrate on deciding what you will do if the negotiation is unsuccessful. The reason you are negotiating at all is that you hope for something better than what might happen if you didn't negotiate. What is your best alternative to those results? Your BATNA has the advantage of being flexible enough to allow you to use your imagination. Instead of ruling out any solution which does not meet your bottom line, you can compare a proposal with your BATNA to see to the level to which it satisfies your interests and needs.

To create your BATNA:

- Invent a list of actions you might conceivably take if no agreement is reached.
- Improve some of the more promising ideas and convert them into practical options.
- Select the option that seems best.
- Work out the other side's BATNA.

Exercise 7.11: Making a BATNA

Group Structure: Seminar groups.
Timing: 30–40 minutes.
Materials: Case studies for each group.

Process: Give each group a set of negotiation briefs and ask them to create a BATNA for each side.

EXAMPLE 1

Terry is an instructor at the Tryhard Tennis School and was given, as were all the instructors, 20 boxes of tennis balls for personal use. The season is coming to an end and Terry, a naturally thrifty person, still has 15 boxes left. The School director has asked for all unused balls to be returned. Terry feels morally obliged to comply, but wants to persuade the director to modify the order.

What is Terry's BATNA?

Explain:

EXAMPLE 2

STUDENT: I know I've got to pass the English exam to get to University but I just can't face it again. I've failed once already and I know I just can't do it. I want you to help me leave school and get a job.

COUNSELLOR: I'll help you as much as I can. I know you're finding the English difficult and I also know that you really want to get to University. Before we talk further maybe you should explore what possibilities there are in the job market for you at the moment. How do your parents feel about your leaving school? Are they willing to keep you are home? Will you have to pay expenses? Take this form which will help you work out how just how much it might cost you if you need to find a flat. In the meantime, I'll have a word with your English teacher to see if there is any extra help which would give you some support. Let's meet again next week to talk further.

In terms of a BATNA, what is the counsellor trying to do?

This ends our investigation into some aspects of managing conflict. The next chapter looks at some issues related to the task of managing other people.

REFERENCES

Fisher, R. & Ury, W. (1982). *Getting to Yes*. Hutchinson.
Huczynski, A. & Buchanan, D. (1991). *Organizational Behaviour*. Prentice Hall.
Jelfs, M. (1982). *Manual for Action*. Action Resources Group.
Salaman, G. (1981). Management development and organisational theory, *Journal of European Industrial Training*, **2** (7): 7–11.
Salaman, G. (1981). *Class and Corporation*. Fontana.
Taylor, L. & Walton, P. (1971). Industrial sabotage: motives and meanings, in *Images of Deviance* (S. Cohen, ed.). Penguin Books.
Thomas, K.W. (1976). Organizational conflict, in *Organizational Behaviour* (S. Kerr, ed.). Columbus, Ohio: Grid.
Vecchio, R.P. (1995). *Organisational Behaviour*. Dryden Press.

8

ORGANISING PEOPLE

The focus of this chapter is people management. Managers are key people in organisations. They are responsible for ensuring that the objectives are met and that resources are appropriately used. Among the resources that any organisation possesses are the people who carry out the various functions necessary to its continuing success. This set of training structures explores the tasks that managers need to carry out in order to make it possible for every member of staff to work to their optimum performance.

SESSION 16: TASKS OF MANAGEMENT AND PROBLEM SOLVING

Training Objectives

1. To identify management activities.
2. To present a model of problem analysis and management.
3. To identify and practise skills of problem management.

Trainer Input

Being a manager means that you are bound to have problems! This first session presents a framework for approaching problem solving. You can use the model personally to help you think through a problem or to guide you through the process of helping someone else. If you have any kind of management function, you will no doubt, from time to time, be called upon to help with the personal or professional problems which affect members of your staff. The following sessions will give you an opportunity to practise some of the skills to help you to stay on track with dealing with difficult situations.

Maintaining achievement of one's full potential requires a range of skills and understanding and this first session focuses, in a general way, on how to think through problems which may be getting in the way of success. The idea we are going to explore is based on a model devised by Gerard Egan (1975), who defines a problem as the difference between what is desired and what actually is happening now. The idea behind the model is to provide a logical process through which a problem situation can be managed as well as possible. We will be looking at this on two levels: taking yourself through the process and helping someone else—perhaps a member of your staff, a colleague or a client. Essentially, the process is the same.

We will split the process into four main stages:

- Exploration and focusing
- New perspectives and goal setting
- Action planning
- Evaluation.

Exploration and Focusing

The aim here is to explore the problem so that all its implications are fully understood and the resources needed to manage it can be gathered together. This mostly means asking a lot of questions in order to determine the history and facts of the situation, to order the problem and effects. The questions should take account of feelings involved without letting them swamp the facts. As the problem is explored it may become obvious that there are many facets to it or there may actually be several problems. If this is the case, the next stage would be to decide which matters should be dealt with first and how the rest should be prioritised.

This is a quick exercise to demonstrate how having a problem can interfere with our ability to be logical. As anxiety and confusion increase, our perceptions become distorted and as stress builds up we feel more and more helpless and then all aspects of our lives suffer—from our personal relationships to organisational objectives.

Exercise 8.1: Seeing the Problem

Group Structure: Whole group.
Timing: 5–10 minutes.

Process: Ask group participants to look around the room, focusing only on whatever they can see that is red in colour. When they have done this for a minute or so, ask them for any observations. These are likely to include the fact that when people focus on one particular colour the others fade into the background. They might also say that the longer they looked the more red they saw. The point of this is when you have a problem (the red) you tend to see everything in relation to the problem.

Awareness of other things is reduced. 'Other things' might include the strengths and experience that you could bring to the problem.

One of the advantages of a logical process for managing problems is that it helps you keep everything relevant in the picture.

What are the relevant skills to this stage?

- *Attention:* If you are helping someone with a problem they need to know that you are giving them attention; this means ensuring that your body language is congruent—good eye contact, open posture, avoidance of distracting behaviour. If you are working on a problem of your own, you need to pay attention to yourself—how you are thinking and feeling and what you are doing and how these things are affecting the situation.

Exercise 8.2: Giving Attention

Group Structure: Work in pairs.
Timing: 10–15 minutes.

Process· Ask participants to get together in pairs, moving their chairs so that each pair is facing each other. Explain that you are going to demonstrate three ways of not giving attention.

Instruct each person to tell the other what they did since the moment they got up this morning—at the same time. After a minute or two, stop the exercise and ask for their observations. They are likely to have noticed that it was easy to get distracted—that if you start listening you tend to stop talking. It is almost impossible to talk and listen at the same time.

Now ask one person in each pair to pretend that they are not at all interested in the other. Instruct the other to talk about a person who has been important to him or her. Let the exercise continue for 3 minutes or so and then stop and ask for people's reactions. You will find that most people feel very upset by the fact that they are being ignored, especially when they are talking about something important to them—even in a game!

Now ask each pair to take it in turns to talk about their feelings about the two exercises. While one is talking, the other should not interrupt but do everything to let the partner know that he or she interested in what the partner is saying. Once again give them time to discuss their observations.

Having thought about the importance of giving attention, let us identify some more skills which are important to this stage.

Notes for the Trainer

At this point, and throughout this input, you could stop and ask the group to brainstorm their ideas about relevant skills. Whether you do so depends on the amount of time you are intending to give to this element in your training schedule. The session could, in fact, be extended to become a training course on its own, and if you are working with trainees or newly appointed managers you may wish to make this an important part of the induction training.

Trainer Input

Here are a range of skills which are good basic communication skills and crucial when trying to help someone think through a problem.

- *Active listening:* This means listening to the verbal and non-verbal communication of the other person. It is as if you are constantly asking yourself: 'What is the core of what this person is trying to communicate? What does the world of this person feel like?'
- *Responding:* This is a way of indicating to people that they have been carefully listened to. It makes it easier for them to believe that you can help them.
- *Basic empathy:* This is probably the most important skill when trying to help someone. Here you are trying to understand more than just the words the person is saying. You are trying to pick up how the person feels and perceives the world. A useful formula is 'You feel . . . because . . . '. For example, 'You feel hurt because she ignores you'; 'You feel annoyed with yourself because you've left it so long'. Phrases like, 'I just want to check I've understood this' or 'You seem to be saying . . . Have I got it right?'; 'Am I correct in thinking that . . . ' will help you check how accurate your empathy is.

We have been talking about using this group of skills when working with another person; it is interesting also to think about how they could be relevant to yourself. How often do we give ourselves time to really listen to ourselves; to notice that the way we are perceiving a problem might be hindering our ability to find a creative solution. One way of doing this would be to speak your thoughts into a tape recorder and then listen as if you were listening to someone else.

Here is a quick exercise to help you key into your own way of thinking.

Exercise 8.3: How Do You Think?

Timing: 10 minutes.

Process: Explain to participants that this exercise is a very quick and personal way to identify how they think. Ask them to keep a notebook and pen handy and relax for a moment. When the group have settled down, ask them to briefly note down anything they find themselves thinking about during the next 5 minutes. Explain that they shouldn't try to think (or not think) about anything in particular but just to notice which thoughts come to them. Also reassure them that they won't have to talk about this to anyone else.

When the time is up, ask people to look at the list of their thoughts and notice any interesting or informative patterns. Are they, for instance, thinking mostly about the past or the future? If so, how much in touch with the present are they? Are their thoughts dominated by one concern or worry—again, does this mean they are losing sight of what else is happening? . . . and so on.

To follow this exercise, here is one which focusing on communication with another person.

Exercise 8.4: Practising Empathy

Group Structure: Work in groups of three.
Timing: 45 minutes for work in threes plus time for general feedback.

Process: When people are in their groups of three ask them to decide which of three roles—person with a problem, helper or observer—they want to play for the first 'round', explaining that everyone will get a chance to play each role.

For the first round the 'person with a problem' should talk about something which is on his or her mind at the moment. You can suggest that people talk about something which is real to them or they can make up a situation. The 'helper' should attempt to empathise, i.e. reflect back in their own words what they are hearing. There is no need to solve the problem at this stage—the exercise is about putting yourself in the shoes of someone else. The observer will listen and watch and then feed back what is noticed.

Each round should take 15 minutes. The process should be repeated so that each person plays each role.

Groups then come together to share learning points.

Gentle probing is also a useful skill to help someone express the problem in specific and concrete terms. For example, someone might say, 'My landlord is treating me badly'. You might first respond with some empathy and follow up with 'What exactly is bothering you . . . ?', 'What precisely is it that has happened? . . . ', 'What is he/she doing? . . . ', 'Is there anything else happening? . . . '. Particularly when time is short, skilful probing can ensure that the person is focused on the problem rather than on side issues which may not be relevant. However, like all skills, probing should be used carefully and with respect, not as a bulldozer to avoid issues which may be important to the person.

Exercise 8.5: Practising Probing

Group Structure: Working in threes.
Timing: 45–50 minutes.

Process: Set up as the previous exercise in threes, with 'person with a problem', 'helper' and 'observer'. Brief the person with the helper role to find out as much about the problem that their partner is presenting by using their probing skills. The observer needs to notice the effect of various interventions: are there any which seem to help or hinder communication? The 'person with a problem' can also give feedback as to how they react to particular interventions.

Repeat the process so that each person gets time to practise.

When the problem has been explored the next task is to decide what to focus on. Problems are very rarely simple—they can have many facets or there can be more than one problem. However, you can only deal with one thing at a time, so ordering the various elements is an important part of the process. To help you, you need to determine:

- Whether there is a crisis—because if there is, that has to be dealt with first.
- Is there a particular order in which it would be sensible to deal with things?
- Is there a particular aspect of the problem which is more important than any other?
- Does any aspect of the problem show promise of being successfully handled by the client or appear to be relatively easy to manage? If there is, this would be a good place to start.
- Is some aspect of the problem arousing deep feelings?
- Are there any legal time limits which operate and would affect any successful resolution?

Exercise 8.6: Putting the First Stage Together

Group Structure: Work in pairs; feedback in large group.
Timing: 40 minutes.
Materials: Exploration and Focusing Question Sheet.

Process: Give each participant a question sheet, suggesting that only one person in the pair looks at it. This person will use the questions to explore a problem which his or her partner presents, using the skills which we have looked at in this session. After 15 minutes, the pair should change roles.

EXPLORATION AND FOCUSING QUESTION SHEET

Instructions: The following list of questions are typical exploration and focusing questions. They are intended to help in building up as complete a picture as possible of the situation the client is facing. When you ask a question, listen carefully to the answer and, before you move on, respond with reflection to check that you have understood and empathise to try to see a little beyond the answer.

Exploration Questions:

- What is actually happening now?
- What is NOT happening?
- How is it affecting you?
- Is it affecting others?
- What are the expectations which others are placing on you?
- Has this happened before?
- What did you do then?
- What would you prefer to be happening?
- What would you have to do to change matters?
- What would things be like if you succeeded?
- Are there any barriers in your way?

- What is the worst that could happen?
- Are you aware of any ways in which you could sabotage yourself?
- Are there any ways in which others could help you?
- Is there anyone in particular who could be of help?

Focusing:

- Is there a time limit?
- Is there a crisis?
- Which aspect of the problem do you have the deepest feelings about?
- What would be easiest to start with?
- What do you want to do?

Notes for the Trainer

Gerard Egan (1975) places great emphasis on the notion of *managing* problems rather than *solving* them. If we believe that our success as a helper can only be measured by the number of problems for which we find solutions, we are bound to experience some level of failure time after time. Some problems are just not soluble. It is more practical to think of helping someone to manage his or her situation better. There is always something we can do—even if it is just a little. For instance, just spending a little time listening empathetically to a troubled person can help that person to feel less alone or misunderstood. That is why the emphasis of the first part of this session has been so much on listening and responding. The training problem is that most people believe they do listen very well already. After all, we are doing it from the moment we are born. The important message of this session is that listening can be developed so that it becomes an important resource in our collection of skills. You may feel that you want to spend more time on this since it is such a crucial communication facility. Here is another exercise which can help to increase people's awareness.

Exercise 8.7: Levels of Listening

Group Structure: Small groups of four or five.
Timing: 15 minutes.

Process: While participants are organising themselves into their small groups, write up on a flip chart the following headings:

INTELLECT   EMOTION   BODY   SPIRIT

Invite participants to think of these four levels of contact and discuss how listening might be experienced at each level. This is a deliberately vague brief and so the discussions might range over various possibilities. The aim is to encourage an analysis of an activity that most of us take for granted—and in fact most of the time only do superficially.

Trainer Input

New Perspectives and Goal Setting

For some people, stage 1 might be enough to carry them forwards. The clarification and insights obtained from exploring and focusing may help them decide on action (or inaction) which they may be both willing and able to carry out themselves. For others it will not be enough, so some guidance on what to do next would be helpful. The main aim of this stage is to move into action that will begin to put into effect the changes that are wanted.

As a first step, it is useful to gain some new perspective on the problem. Because it is very easy to get into a repetitive way of thinking about a problem, it is possible to get to a point where no new thoughts can be created. When this stage is reached, a feeling of helplessness often sets in. It is most helpful, in this situation, to have a new perspective which will help create the energy needed to take action.

There are various ways of doing this. For instance:

Making Connections
If a problem has many facets or a lengthy history it is useful to try to look for connections which will help to make sense of what is happening.

Challenging
It is possible that one's perception of the situation may be too narrow or distorted. Remember the 'Looking for Red' exercise. In this case your aim is to develop a wider, more objective or more realistic perspective in order to set helpful goals. You can do this by:

- *Sharing information:* Sometimes a problem is made worse by the fact that the necessary information is not known. If you are helping someone else, you may be in a good position to provide such information which will often show the situation in a new light. If you are on your own you may need to do some research by talking to others or reading relevant literature.
- *Advanced empathy:* The empathy we have explored so far can be further developed. You can share your guesses about the person and the situation. For instance:
  - 'The problem doesn't seem to be just about the redundancy payment but also about how the situation is affecting your marriage.' (*Presenting a bigger picture*)

— 'I am wondering if you are not only sad about your loss, but angry too.' (*Clarifying implications*)

— 'From all you've said about your wife, it seems that you are not certain about the divorce. You haven't actually said it but I am wondering if you are regretting the action you took.' (*Drawing possible conclusions*)

— 'I wonder if it's possible that your neighbour took you too literally—that she saw what you said as sarcasm rather than a joke.' (*Pointing out something which may have been overlooked*)

— 'It seems that you have been in this kind of situation several times before in your life.' (*Identifying themes*)

Challenging in this way can be very stimulating in that new ways of thinking about things can result, but you have to be careful not to sound critical or accusatory. If you decide to challenge in this way, deliver your challenge extremely tentatively so that the person you are challenging knows that he or she can refute your idea without making things worse between you.

Exercise 8.8: Challenging

Group Structure: Whole group or smaller workshop groups.
Timing: 20 minutes.
Materials: Case study sheets for each person or each group.

Process: Give each person (or group) a list of possible statements made by a client. (You can create a list of your own, if you want, to give examples of situations participants might actually come across.) Ask them to devise a challenging response. They should be able to explain the purpose behind the challenge they choose.

CHALLENGING PRACTICE SHEET

Imagine that these statements have been made to you. Devise a possible challenging response. Be prepared to explain your purpose behind the response you choose.

A. I've never been able to talk to people. I get very tongue-tied and can never think of what to say.

B. My parents are to blame for everything! If they'd looked after me properly when I was a kid I wouldn't be in this state now.

C. It's hopeless. I'll never understand computers. I think I'll have to look for another kind of job because I don't see how I could ever do what's expected of me now.

Challenging someone else is somewhat easier than challenging oneself. However, finding ways of challenging yourself might be just what you need to help you forward.

Exercise 8.9: Challenge Yourself.

Timing: 20 minutes.
Materials: Common Beliefs Sheet for each participant.

Process: Hand out the worksheet and explain that it lists some very common beliefs, all of which tend to be too extreme to be really true. Ask participants to remember a recent time when they felt under stress and to identify any of the statements which might have been influencing their response at the time.

COMMON BELIEFS

- I must be liked/loved by everyone.
- Everything I do must be perfect
- It is always better to do things more quickly.
- Other people should behave perfectly.
- I cannot control what happens to me.
- Not facing up to difficulties is easier than dealing with them.
- Everything I do should be 'right'.
- I should try to avoid conflict whatever the cost.
- It is not possible for people to change.
- It is a disaster that the world is not perfect.
- People are too fragile to be faced with the truth.
- If I start something, I always have to finish it.
- My happiness depends on other people.
- Other people's happiness depends on me.
- Crises are always disastrous and nothing good ever comes from them.
- If I try hard enough I will find the perfect partner/job/life.
- I should be able to cope with my problems on my own; not to do so is weakness.
- Other people should be able to cope with their problems on their own.
- Every problem has the 'right' solution; I just have to keep searching for it.

If you identified with any of these beliefs try challenging this way of thinking, exchange the 'shoulds' and 'oughts' for preferences. Rewrite those beliefs as more realistic statements.

Summarising

At a number of points throughout the session it is useful to summarise the principal points that have come up and the progress which is being made.

Exercise: 8.10: Practising Summarising

Group Structure: Work in pairs; feedback to whole group.
Timing: 10–20 minutes.

Process: As a quick summarising exercise, ask participants to work in pairs to produce a summary of the session so far. The summaries can be presented to the whole group so that people can see how perceptions and memories can vary.

Self-Disclosure

There are times when describing your own experience will help someone understand their problem better. It is an intervention which needs to be used sparingly because you don't want to distract the person from his or her own efforts. An example of a potentially helpful disclosure 'You seem to be feeling very distressed that you haven't recovered from the death of your wife. I remember that when I was bereaved it took me two years to begin come to terms with it.'

Confrontation

There are times when we overlook discrepancies which are obvious to an onlooker. Pointing this out to someone can give a new perspective to the situation. For instance, it can be easy to forget they have skills which have helped you through similar troubles in the past. Or you may be seeing the problem as one for which another person is totally to blame when, in fact, they may be responsible at least in part. Just like other skills in this section, this is to be used carefully with others. People don't usually respond positively if they feel criticised, put down or patronised.

Exercise 8.11: New Ways for New Perspectives

Group Structure: Brainstorm session.
Timing: 5 minutes.

Process: Ask participants to call out any other ways they can think of providing a new perspective. Some possibilities are:

- Reading.
- Talking to others who have experienced similar problems.
- Talking to others who have not experienced similar problems (sometimes the 'outsider' sees most of the game!).
- Relating the problem to some theoretical framework (e.g. a problem of communication between staff can be seen more clearly in the light of the ideas about communication in Transactional Analysis; a block in decision making can be explored through the concept of a problem management model).
- Organising training around the specific problem area.

We have now moved towards the next stage in this model—that of goal setting. This is where the action really begins! Sometimes thinking and talking about a problem is enough to show the way to better management—but often it isn't. If it isn't, then decisions need to be made as to what needs to be done. Goals are the actions which need to be accomplished in order to manage the problem situation, or some part of it, more effectively.

Goals should be stated clearly. They need to be

- *Specific and concrete:* It is tempting to believe that others are responsible for the problem—and for the solution. Making a goal specific means stating it as if it is achievable—by you. If, for instance, you stated your problem as 'I know all my problems are due to the terrible education I had. When I was at school, teachers weren't interested in helping me and my parents were too busy to take time with me', you are essentially presenting an insoluble situation. You cannot change the past. However, things sound different if you say, 'My knowledge of science is not good enough to carry me further in my career. I want to continue on this particular path, so I need to think how to increase my knowledge.'
- *Measurable or verifiable:* It is important to have a sense of how things were before a change took place and how they are after it has been achieved. This enables change to be identified and experienced as a reward, and gives you proof that your efforts are worth while. If tangible proof is not possible, a record of changing thoughts and feelings can serve as a very positive measure of movement. 'I only scraped through O-level science at school and I would like to study it at least to A-level standard.'
- *Realistic:* Setting a goal which, although challenging, is within your abilities and resources is vital. Too often, people fail to succeed because they have set their sights too high. 'I expect to obtain a Science Degree by next year' is a possible example!
- *Adequate:* On the other hand, you need to be sure that what you are deciding to do will actually make a difference. 'I'll think about it next year' is probably not likely to have a great effect now.

- *Within a reasonable time frame:* The previous example also shows the importance of giving yourself a reasonable time frame within which to achieve your goals. If you give yourself too long, you will lose the impetus; if you leave yourself too short of time, you are likely to get stressed or frustrated because you cannot succeed.
- *Related to the general problem:* Many problems have different angles and there is nothing more frustrating than trying to do several things at once. When you set goals, select some aspect of the problem which, although specific in itself, is related to the problem as a whole. It is easier to succeed with small, achievable goals—and nothing breeds success better than success! Succeeding at a small goal will give you energy and motivation to try something bigger and so you will proceed through the various aspects of the situation.
- *Valuable:* To stay motivated, you need some personal investment in the goals you create. This means ensuring that whatever you are deciding to do carries positive value for you. The problem in helping others through this process is that we tend to have different yardsticks as to our values. You could, for instance choose a goal because it is considered to be socially worth while or someone else thinks it will be good for you, rather than because you feel it is a good thing. If you do, you are likely to lose your initial enthusiasm and energy.

Exercise 8.12: Goal-Setting Practice

Group Structure: Workshop groups followed by feedback.
Timing: 45 minutes.
Materials: Case study scenarios.

Process: Give out prepared scenarios to groups. Explain that they are very briefly sketched so the group can flesh them out with details if they want. The objective is for each group to come up with a set of goals for each problem and to have tested them by the criteria described in the session. The discussion should focus on the process of setting the goals rather than the content of the problems.

EXAMPLES OF CASE STUDY SCENARIOS
1. Sally, a designer, has three children aged under 10; she has worked part time since the birth of her first child and now needs to increase her earning power. She wants to get back into full-time work but feels that potential employers will be put off by her young family.
2. John, who is 50 and the manager of a social work department, recently had a minor heart attack and has recovered well. However, although

he is back at work he feels very anxious that his health will break down again. He finds himself avoiding confrontations that he knows he should see through and realises that he is not working to his full potential.

3. Davina, manager of a national voluntary organisation, is worried about conflicts which have arisen between individuals in the organisation. She is not sure of the reasons why these conflicts have arisen, but now people are taking sides, complaining about each other, refusing to work with each other and so on. The atmosphere in the organisation has become very unpleasant and the quality of work is suffering.

Action Planning

Action planning is the third stage of this model and it is the time to move from talking and thinking to acting. Having decided upon the goals which should help make the necessary changes, we need to generate as many options for action as possible. Facing a long-standing problem can be exhausting and leave little energy for thinking of new solutions. What can be useful at this point is a brainstorm to generate new possibilities.

Exercise 8.13: Brainstorming Options

Group Structure: Whole group.
Timing: 5 minutes.

Process: Taking one of the examples which participants have been working on during the goal setting session, ask people to call out any possible way of achieving that particular goal. Remember that brainstorming is intended to be a free flow of ideas, so don't let the group start discussing the feasibility of any particular idea. Just note down anything that comes up—however absurd it may seem.

For example, one of Davina's (see above) goals might be to find out how the problem started. The brainstorm list might look like:

- Send everyone a letter explaining your concerns.
- Invite everyone to a meeting.
- Employ an outside consultant.
- Talk to everyone individually.
- Throw an office party.
- Bribe people to talk about each other.

- Place hidden tape recorders everywhere.
- Spend time hidden in the loo to hear the gossip.
- Talk to other managers who have had similar problems.
- Let things ride and hope everything will sort itself out.
- Go away on holiday.
- Find another job.

When the list is complete, consider each item as to whether it would be practical or desirable or not. Its aim is to give someone several options so that if the first does not seem to be working, he or she can move on to the second on the list rather than feel a failure.

Here are some questions that are useful for you to ask yourself when considering taking action:

- Are there any people who could help me achieve this goal?
- Are there any places from which I could get help?
- Are their any organisations available to help?
- Are there any ready-made programmes that could help me?

The criteria for choosing a particular course of action are the same as for a goal—concrete, specific, measurable, verifiable, realistic, adequate, within a reasonable time frame, related to a general problem, and valuable.

We are now at the stage when you (or the other person) are taking action. Although nobody else can actually take responsibility for the action which is necessary, support from others can be very therapeutic. You might offer support to the person you are helping, or ask for support if you are taking the action yourself. Sometimes it's good to know that there is someone rooting for you if you are trying to achieve something.

The last stage of this problem management model is often forgotten, but it is important.

Evaluation

Evaluation is important because:

- If things are not progressing well, you need to stop and think why.
- If any course of action is going wrong, then it is important to ask 'What's going wrong and what can be done to correct things?'
- If your success is not complete, or as efficient or quick as expected, then the question is 'What can I do to improve my progress?'
- If the problem has been managed absolutely successfully, evaluation is still useful and should be based on the question, 'What else would the strategies, skills and techniques that I have used be useful for addressing?'

- If there is no end product to give evidence of your effectiveness, then evaluating how problems are managed will make it clear whether your objectives are being achieved.
- Evaluation makes it easier for you to present your work to the outside world in such a way that it will be valued. Making global statements about the usefulness of the work is not enough to prove that a service is a valuable one.

Notes for the Trainer

The previous session can stand alone as an introduction to problem management and can be extended by including more practice exercises. Case studies could be presented so that participants could practise approaching problems in this particular way. The session can also be modified to provide basic training for counsellors, advice givers, lawyers, doctors—anyone in fact whose work involves helping people to manage their problems better. The aim of the next session is to identify the range of other skills which managers need.

The session, while focusing on delegation, starts with a mention of goal setting which is the foundation for the other activities. If you are following on from Session 11 there will be no need to do any more than remind people of the process. If you are starting from this point, you will probably need to include some of the goal-setting input and exercises from Session 11.

SESSION 17: GOAL SETTING AND DELEGATION

Training Objectives

1. To explore the place of goal setting and delegation in the range of management skills.
2. To identify criteria of readiness for delegation.
3. To describe basic delegation strategies.
4. To practise delegation skills.

Trainer Input

We have looked at the need for managers to be able to manage problems as well as people and now we are moving on to look at other activities that managers can employ to achieve their aims. Managers depend for their success on the performance of those people working with or for them. This means requiring people to be at their very best all of the time. There are times, of course, when people do turn in an extraordinary performance, perhaps exceeding all expectations, but this often occurs by chance. Many managers use their intuition to motivate people—with varying levels of success. The principle behind these sessions is that it is possible to motivate people to give of their best most of the time without depending on intuition or chance. We are going to be exploring how optimum performance by individual members of staff can be planned, discussed and reinforced by a manager for each member of staff.

Most organisations have structures which can be used to enhance people's performance in their job. Examples are goal setting, delegation, training, coaching, counselling and appraisals. A manager can use these activities in a logical sequence to maximise the opportunities they offer.

The sequence I am suggesting is

DEFINING EXPECTATIONS AND SETTING GOALS
(formally or informally establishing direction and clarifying expectations)
↓
DELEGATING
(assigning work)
↓
TRAINING AND DEVELOPMENT
(teaching job skills and preparing people for the future)
↓
COACHING AND COUNSELLING
(helping people solve both work-and non-work-related problems that affect their performance)
↓
PERFORMANCE APPRAISAL
(primary focus on the improvement of employee's future performance)

We have already explored the first of these, goal setting, while learning about the problem management model. It is the way to create a good foundation for the following developmental activities. Goal setting, which is focused on motivation, should state:

● Who will achieve the goal.
● What action will be taken.
● What the measurable result will be.
● The target date for completion.

The goals should emphasise results over activities—for example, attending a meeting is an *activity*; creating a new pricing structure is a *result*. They should be measurable, challenging but achievable and linked to other organisational goals. The goals should be mutually agreed upon and subject to periodic review and revision.

Exercise 8.14: Good Goals

Group Structure: Work in pairs, threes or buzz groups.
Timing: 15 minutes.

Process: Having given an input about what makes a useful goal, ask the groups to write out three or four examples. These can then be discussed and checked against the criteria.

Having set goals with a particular person, let's consider the next motivational development—delegation.

Exercise 8.15: Defining Delegation:

Group Structure: Brainstorm
Timing: 5 minutes.

Process: Write the word DELEGATION on the flip chart and invite the group to call out any words that come to mind to describe their response.

Notes for the Trainer

This quick exercise will give you an idea of how the group views the process of delegation. Some people have a very negative experience; others feel they could do more. One of the points you want to get over is that the key to successful delegation is an accurate perception concerning a person's readiness to perform a specific task. Negative experiences are often linked to people being given tasks for which they are not trained or ready. The problem for managers who themselves have had negative experiences is that they are often very wary of delegating to others.

Trainer Input

Delegation can be a very powerful motivator. The key to success is to be able to judge when someone is ready in terms of their competence and commitment. Readiness can be divided into the following stages:

Stage 1: Being able to perform a single carefully delineated task.

Stage 2: In addition to being able to perform the task, to be able to anticipate manager's future needs.

Stage 3: Able to participate in planning, problem solving and evaluation of task.

Stage 4: Being able to see through the complete task from start to finish without supervision and reinforcement.

Exercise 8.16: Ready for Delegation?

Group Structure: Small workshop groups.
Timing: 30 minutes.

Process: Ask groups to discuss aspects of their present job which could be delegated and then choose two or three to work on together. Ask them to define the skills, knowledge and/or attitudes the delegatee should be able to demonstrate at each level. When the whole group meets together, the discussion should focus on matters such as how they would determine the readiness of the delegatee.

Here are some basic guidelines to good delegation:

- For any task you are considering delegating, first evaluate the delegatee's developmental level and probable stage of readiness.
- Be sure you fully understand the task to be delegated.
- Divide the task into segments that could fit the four stages of readiness.
- Explain clearly what you want done, how you want it done, when it is to be completed and with whom the delegatee is to interact.
- Show trust and support throughout the process.
- Organise progress 'checkpoints'.
- Review work jointly and reinforce tasks which are well done.

Exercise 8.17: Practising Delegation Skills

Group Structure: Role play in pairs (with audio tapes) or threes (with observer); review of learning points by whole group.
Timing: Up to one hour.

Process: Participants can continue to work on the example they used in Exercise 8.16 or think of a different one. (You can provide pre-written case studies but real-life examples are probably more useful as practical learning situations.)

Each person should spend 10–15 minutes preparing for a meeting with their 'delegatee'. The person role playing the delegatee needs to be briefed in advance as to his or her level of readiness, etc., so that an appropriate response can be given.

The delegation sessions are then role played; if people are working in pairs, they can audio-tape the session for review; if in threes, someone will always be in the 'observer' role.

The delegation process is one of the prime tools which a manager has of helping some grow and develop on the job. Another important consideration is that, apart from helping others to grow, you are helping yourself. You cannot do everything yourself—you need the people in your team to help you, and although good delegation may take time to set up, you will benefit in the long run.

SESSION 18: TRAINING AND DEVELOPMENT

Training Objectives

1. Defining the terms 'training' and 'development'.
2. Analysing training needs.
3. Preparing an individual training and development programme.

Trainer Input

The third strategy for helping people achieve their best performance involves training and development which might be needed for someone to accomplish the goals they have set and the new tasks which may have been delegated.

Exercise 8.18: Defining Terms

Group Structure: Whole group.
Timing: 5–10 minutes.
Materials: Flip chart with words 'Coaching', 'Training' and 'Development' written up.

Process: Taking each word in turn, ask participants to call out any functions which they think are covered by that word.

Notes for the Trainer

This brainstorm is likely to show that the words coaching, training and development are often used as if they were interchangeable. In helping managers to clearly define the various strategies open to them, it is useful to differentiate between these activities. Clarifying the difference between them will help managers to make decisions regarding the progress of individual staff members. If no clear definition results from the brainstorm you can, at this point, provide one.

Trainer Input

Coaching

As we start looking at this next strategy, let's get our terms clear. You can use coaching to help someone improve their job performance. If, for instance, a person isn't very good at giving instruction to staff for which they are responsible, coaching may well be an appropriate intervention. It is less formal than training and usually happens near to the time the problem arises. Whereas training involves setting objectives, repetition, review and so on, coaching is briefer. However brief or informal, it is useful to give it the same careful consideration which we have been giving to the various managerial options we have explored so far.

The overall purpose here is to help someone improve performance or change behaviour and can be seen as a three-stage process.

Stage 1: Analysis of Problem
Spending time thinking systematically about the nature of dissatisfaction which has led you to think of coaching. Try to determine precisely what the problem is about—is it lack of skill, knowledge or a personality problem? Questions like, 'Does X know that he/she is not performing satisfactorily?'; 'What are the factors which might be influencing X?'; 'What are the implications of taking no action?'; and so on.

Stage 2: Face-to-Face Coaching Session
If the answers you get lead you to believe that coaching is going to be the best intervention, you need to set up a session with the person. The meeting could take this format:

1. You explain the purpose of the session (e.g. 'I want to talk with you about your case recording which doesn't seem to be following the organisation's guidelines').
2. You ask the person to share his or her perception on the problem (e.g. 'How are you finding this requirement?').
3. You describe your perspective (e.g. 'This is what I've noticed').

4. Jointly compare perspectives (e.g. 'We seem to have different views about this').
5. Explain the changes you suggest; giving relevant information or demonstration (e.g. 'I would like to go through the guidelines with you and show how your recordings could fit them').
6. Ask the person what he or she wants from you (e.g. 'Is there any reason you would find this problematic? Can I help in any way?').
7. Jointly decide how to make the changes (e.g. 'What's the best way to proceed?').
8. Set date for review (e.g. 'Let's meet in a month to see how things are going').

Stage 3: Review
The review meeting can be used to check on whether the changes have been made, to resolve any problems standing in the way and to give positive reinforcement to success.

Training, as I've implied, is a more formal and often lengthier process to give people the skills they need to carry out the job they are expected to do at present. For instance, if your job requires you to coach staff to enable them to improve their performance, you may need to have some training in coaching skills.

Development is more focused on the future. It is the offering of learning opportunities to prepare someone for roles and responsibilities they have in the future. Development is often tied in with organisational and individual objectives. For instance, if the organisation is planning to offer a legal service next year, members of staff who are expected or wish to be involved may require a chance to develop their abilities in this field.

Having clarified what coaching, training and development mean, the next step is to think through what kinds of needs would trigger these responses.

Exercise 8.19: Coaching, Training or Development?

Group Structure: Small discussion groups
Timing: 10 minutes

Process: Suggest that participants list the kind of problems that could be met through the three difference strategies.

Training
We have explored coaching in some detail. Let's now look at training. The best way to begin analysing training needs is to clarify what the job actually

entails. This exercise will help you to do that. If you have a formal job description, you can use it to refer to while you are doing the exercise.

Exercise 8.20: Identifying Training Needs through the Job Description

Group Structure: Individual work, followed by work in pairs.
Timing: 30 minutes.

Process: There are three steps to this exercise. Ask participants to make a list of the elements which make up the job under consideration (their present job or one they are aiming for in the future). Then rate the list in order of importance to the total job. The next step is to make a list of the skills and knowledge required to carry out the items on the list. The third step is for each person to rate his or her current level of skill or ability to carry out the task by using a simple numerical system: 0 = none; 10 = absolute.

Working in pairs, participants can then identify specific training activities which will meet their needs.

Identifying needs is the first step; delivering the training is the next. Here is a four-stage guide for providing training for individuals or groups of staff:

Stage 1: Preparation
Firstly, find out what the potential trainee already knows about the job and talk about the benefits of training. Identify the conditions and resources that would be necessary for a successful outcome and make sure these are available.

Stage 2: Presentation
This is where you (or the trainer) demonstrates or describes the skills or knowledge deemed necessary. Instruction should be clear and complete, one point at a time with constant checking on how the training is being understood.

Stage 3: Practising
This is the stage at which the new skills are tried out by the trainee either alone or under your guidance. The role of the trainer is to ask questions and correct mistakes until you are sure the person is confident in performing the task.

Stage 4: Review
Here trainees are on their own—doing the job. Your role is to review progress,

continuing to help when necessary but aiming to tail off your involvement as confidence increases.

Exercise 8.21: Practising Delivering Training

Group Structure: Small workshop groups.
Timing: Up to 50 minutes.
Materials: Results from previous exercise or prepared case study.

Process: As material for this practice, participants can use the results from the previous exercise, an example from their current situation or a prepared case study. Using the guidelines given, ask people to design a training programme to increase the knowledge/skills with the highest ratings.

SESSION 19: COUNSELLING

Training Objectives

1. To define counselling as a management initiative
2. To identify management skills required
3. To provide opportunities for the practice of skills

Trainer Input

The next phase of this process moves into counselling skills. Firstly, let's be clear what we are talking about.

Exercise 8.22: What is Counselling?

Group Structure: Whole group brainstorm.
Timing: 5–10 minutes.
Materials: Flip chart with 'Counselling as a Management Activity' written up.

Process: Ask people to call out any words or phrases that come to mind to describe what they feel about counselling as a management skill.

Notes for the Trainer

Counselling is a very wide-ranging concept. It can mean anything between giving someone advice about a practical problem and deep, long-standing psychotherapy. People often have very strong views about its appropriateness as a management activity, anxious perhaps that it can be deeply personal and intimate. It would be inappropriate for a manager to engage in psychotherapy with a member of staff. Apart from anything else, it is likely to be very time and energy consuming. However, sometimes a person's work performance is affected by their personal problems, and at these times a manager may need to take on the role of the accepting, objective counsellor in order to help the person improve the situation.

The training of a professional counsellor is often structured over several years. The training we are considering here is geared for the kind of 'first-aid', brief-intervention counselling which is most appropriate for managers to offer. If the situation turns out to require more than this, the manager is likely to refer the person to a professional counsellor who can offer long-term help.

You will find that some of the exercises and inputs described in Chapter 2 would be very appropriate for inclusion in this session.

Trainer Input

The main aim of counselling is to help people make and act on choices to help them live more happily and resourcefully. This means helping the person find his or her own solutions rather than taking on the problem as your own. When you sense that something is troubling a member of staff to the point where it is affecting that person's work you can invite him or her to talk about it. Most people try to keep their problems away from work, but it is difficult to separate one's personal and work lives to that extent if the problems are burdensome and complex. Having a problem, as we saw in the first session of this chapter, tends to colour the whole of one's perception of life.

Exercise 8.23: Noticing the Problem

Group Structure: Whole group brainstorm.
Timing: 5–10 minutes.
Materials: Flip chart.

Process: Ask participants what signs and symptoms might lead them to think that a member of staff might have some personal problem which he or she is finding difficult to manage, and write up the list. Examples might include:

- Sudden change in behaviour or habit (e.g. someone who is usually very punctual arriving late).
- Someone appearing not to want to leave at night.
- Loss of ability to concentrate.
- Inappropriate responses.
- Tearfulness.
- Outbursts of anger . . . and so on.

If you do notice such signs, what can you do? You should first open an opportunity to talk, saying something like: 'I have the feeling that something is troubling you. I'd be happy to make some time if you feel like talking about it.' It is important to leave the person with the choice of talking to you or not; you certainly cannot force the issue.

If the person you are concerned about does respond, the next stage would be to help him or her to define the problem. The questioning exercise earlier in this chapter is very helpful here. The key is to ask questions which will help focus on the issues underlying the situation. It may take some time; it can be difficult for someone to talk about more personal matters, especially if they are feeling embarrassed or in some way at fault for the situation.

After this clarification, you can help the person develop alternatives for action. Asking 'What might happen if . . . ' is a useful question to begin an exploration of the implications of possible solutions. You need to be careful about offering advice or imposing your solution—tempting though it might be. The most important element of the counselling approach is that people with problems take the responsibility for their decisions. If you give advice which they choose to take there are two possibilities.

1. If the advice works and the situation improves, the person has learned that the thing to do when you have a problem is to find someone who can tell you what to do.
2. If the advice doesn't work, then you will likely be blamed! So hold off advice-giving if at all possible.

In many situations this kind of discussion will, at the very least, provide the person with the relief of knowing that someone is trying to help; sometimes just talking about a problem is enough to reduce some of the strain of trying to keep it to yourself. The process itself can also foster a positive, co-operative relationship between you and staff.

However, there are some issues which you need to think about if and when you decide to use this strategy.

One important matter is that of confidentiality. Professional counselling always take place within an understood framework of confidentiality. Counsellors will inform clients about the level of confidentiality they can offer, and work strictly within those boundaries. However, it is more problematic when you are counselling someone with whom you already have a relationship. For instance, meetings need to be set up so that the purpose is not obvious to other staff members. You must be careful that confidential and personal information never slips out in conversation. People have the right not to be gossiped about.

Exercise 8.24: Counselling Skills

Group Structure: Workshop groups.
Timing: 10 minutes.
Materials: Flip-chart, pen and paper for each group.

Process: Ask participants to list on the flip-chart paper the skills and attitudes necessary for effective counselling. When the groups have finished, the sheets can be displayed on the wall and discussed.

You could categorise these skills into groups of particular responses:

- *Evaluative*—in which you make judgements.
- *Interpretative*—which is more like 'reading between the lines' and using intuition.
- *Supportive*—in which you offer psychological and actual support and understanding.
- *Probing*—in which you question to get more or deeper information.
- *Accepting*—which means giving a non-directive, non-evaluative response which reflects back to the speaker what he or she is saying.

All of these responses would be appropriate in particular situations, but none of them would be right for every occasion. However, each of us tends to have our own particular style of responding which is probably a mixture of some of the above. What would be most useful would be the ability to feel comfortable in each style so that we could adapt our approach to the nature of the situation.

Exercise 8.25: Counselling Skills Practice

Group Structure: Work in threes with one person acting as observer, or in pairs with audio or video tape to be used for feedback, followed by group discussion.

Timing: 1 hour.
Materials: Case study briefs as starting points for role plays; recording sheets for observer.

Process: Participants, working in pairs and using the briefs they have been given as starting points, role play a counselling session. One person takes the counsellor's role and the other develops the brief he or she has been given. If participants prefer, the 'client' can use something which is real—perhaps a problem which has been on his or her mind lately. In many ways, this is preferable because the person does not have to make up a coherent story and also because some real help might be forthcoming. Observers will mark each counselling intervention on the sheet, categorising them as far as they can. If tapes are used, this part of the exercise will be done after the counselling role plays.

What people should look for are patterns of response: are there responses which are being over-used or under-used? An important point to make is that Rogers (1951) said that if we use any one response for 40% of the time, we are seen as that type of person.

EXAMPLES OF COUNSELLING EXERCISE BRIEFS

1. *Newly appointed manager:* I'm a very ambitious person; I really want to get on. I know that this might mean treading on a few people's toes, but you can't worry too much about people's finer feelings, can you? I intend to succeed here.

2. *Female interviewee:* I have just finished a 2-year diploma at Management College which I feel has equipped me well to take on a post here. I had to compete with men on the course and I feel I was more than a match for them.

3. *Man in his fifties:* I started off hoping I would make top management, but as I've got older it's become less important. It's my family who are most important to me and the time I spend with them is what I value most.

4. When I started here I thought I would make a lot of friends but that doesn't seem to have happened. I enjoy my job but I would like more of a social life.

5. I don't know why I've come to see you. On the surface everything is fine; I've got good feedback from my line manager and I know I'm doing the job well. But I worry all the time as to whether I'm going to be able to keep it up. Everything at home is fine, too. There's really no specific problem I can put my finger on, but I have this awful feeling all the time.

OBSERVATION SHEET

Note to observers: Watch and listen to the 'counsellor'; each time he or she makes an intervention mark it off on this sheet according to the category you think it most nearly matches. Here is a guide to the categories:

- *Evaluative:* makes judgements, gives opinions.
- *Interpretive:* uses intuition, hunches, interprets.
- *Supportive:* agrees, backs up, offers help, approves, encourages.
- *Probing:* questions, asks for more/deeper information.
- *Understanding:* empathy, accepting, non-judgmental.

OBSERVATION RECORD

Name of 'Counsellor': ....

EVALUATIVE:

□□□□□□□□□□□□□□□□□□□□□□□□□□

INTERPRETIVE:

□□□□□□□□□□□□□□□□□□□□□□□□□□

SUPPORTIVE:

□□□□□□□□□□□□□□□□□□□□□□□□□□

PROBING:

□□□□□□□□□□□□□□□□□□□□□□□□□□

UNDERSTANDING:

□□□□□□□□□□□□□□□□□□□□□□□□□□

SESSION 20: APPRAISAL

Training Objectives

1. To define the purpose and activity of appraisal.
2. To determine appraisal strategies.
3. To identify skills.

Trainer Input

Appraisal is a word which has caused many a strong manager to shiver and many a perfectly competent employee to tremble. The staff appraisal system is often the main tool with which an organisation or a manager measures the effectiveness of staff. However, if the other strategies which we have explored have been attended to carefully, appraisal becomes a natural and constructive development, to which staff look forward. It forms the last link in this chain of management strategies for motivating staff.

Exercise 8.26: What is Appraisal For?

Group Structure: Group brainstorm.
Timing: Up to 5 minutes.
Materials: Flip chart with question 'What is Appraisal For?' written up.

Process: Ask the group to give their answer to the question, listing as many functions as possible.

To be really effective, we need to make sure that the appraisal interview is not overloaded with too many objectives. As we see from the brainstorm, appraisal can be used by the organisation to:

(a) provide a database of information about people in the organisation with regard to their skills, achievements and expectations
(b) provide a mechanism for the proper assessment of performance so that staff can be appropriately rewarded;

and by the individual to:

(c) help the person assess performance and identify personal strengths and weaknesses
(d) assist in the setting of objectives for personal or job development and to plan ways of meeting them
(e) provide an opportunity for the identification of problems and options for solutions.

As you can see, some of these objectives are incompatible, so no appraisal structure can contain them all. Some are related to development of the individual and others provide the organisation with a control mechanism. For instance, if the system is linked to reward for achievement, it is unlikely that staff members will be open to admitting any weaknesses. So (b) is incompatible with (c) and possibly (e). Charles Handy (1976) notes a study in General Electric (GE) which showed that individuals actually performed worse twelve weeks after their appraisal interview on those aspects of the job for which they received most criticism. In that study the majority finished with less self-esteem than when they started. Low self-esteem often leads to attempts to justify the past, refute accusations and reduce the importance of the process, the job or the manager. Praise is ineffective unless close in time to the behaviour. General commendation is discounted as politeness. So (c) does not necessarily help towards (d).

You might be wondering why appraisal is needed at all; after all, if the previous phases have been managed well, what is left to achieve? It is true that in a good system there will be no surprises in an appraisal discussion.

Any problems which have arisen would have already been discussed and managed so the appraisal interview is best seen as an opportunity to formally discuss the person's past performance and those problems that may hinder his or her success in the future. Career planning, salary review and formal goal setting are best left for other occasions.

As in the counselling process which we have just examined, good appraisal also rests on three conditions:

- An open, trusting relationship based on respect for each other between manager and staff member.
- A willingness to engage in joint inquiry.
- A problem-managing approach rather than a judgemental, punitive approach.

Many of the things we have already said about effective communication apply here. The GE examples show that criticism only improves performance when it is given with genuine respect, when it is related to specific instances and when the 'criticised' trusts and respects the 'criticiser'.

Exercise 8.27: Constructive appraisal

Group Structure: Small working groups.
Timing: 20 minutes.
Materials: Flip-chart, paper and pens for each group.

Process: Firstly, ask people to share their experiences of appraisal, taking, if possible, a good experience and a bad experience. Then tell them to make two lists on their sheets: one headed 'What contributes to Good Appraisal' and What contributes to Bad Appraisal'. These lists then form the basis of a general discussion.

Appraisal
The word appraisal suggests analysis and evaluation by the manager of the employee. However, let's not forget the value of self-appraisal. Even if no formal opportunity for self-appraisal exists in the organisation, the manager can ask the staff member to reflect on his or her own performance either before or during the appraisal session.

Here is one suggestion for a structured appraisal session which includes opportunities for self- as well as manager-appraisal.

Stage 1: Review
In this first part of the interview the job description will form the basis of the discussion which should focus on the main tasks carried out, expected results

and what actually happened. Any confusion relating to the job description or organisational objectives can be clarified at this point.

Your role is to listen, check understanding, empathise as far as possible and note any issues which need further exploration. To do this well, you need to be able to create an atmosphere in which the person feels comfortable and confident enough to talk freely.

Stage 2: Appreciation

When the review is finished, you need to single out tasks well done to offer praise. Praise should be linked to specific achievements, improvements and/or any specific qualities which have been discerned in the period under review. You can also encourage the person to talk about what has given him or her most satisfaction during this period.

Stage 3: Problem Solving

This is when any tasks not done so well (or at all) should be discussed. The four 'R's is a useful formula for constructive criticism. The process is as follows:

1. *Report:* Describe the specific behaviour which causes the problem without linking it to personal insults or general comments (e.g. 'I notice you have been late twice this week'; 'You haven't completed your case recordings'; 'You have spoken brusquely to some clients').
2. *Relate:* Describe how it affects you; what you think and feel in relation to it, without blaming the person for your response (e.g. 'I am concerned because the staff rota has been affected'; 'I am finding it difficult to complete my own objectives without the information'; 'I am worried that clients are not getting the service they deserve').
3. *Request:* Tell the person what it is you want them to do differently. (e.g. 'I would like you to arrive on time'; 'I would like the case recordings given to me by the end of today'; 'I would prefer it if you took more time talking to clients').
4. *Result:* Explain what you think the result of their co-operation (or non-co-operation) will be (e.g. 'The work of the department will be easier to organise'; 'I will be able to meet my targets'; 'Clients will feel more respected and our service reputation will improve').

The person can also be encouraged to identify and talk through the reasons for any problems and how he or she thinks improvements might be achieved. A problem-solving approach should be used for this part of the interview, using the model we explored earlier.

Stage 4: Goal Setting

Now is the time to set goals on agreed targets for the following period. This part of the interview should be recorded and a copy of the record agreed and kept by both parties. This record will serve as a useful resource for the next interview, as well as a schedule which can be worked to.

Stage 5: Conclusion
Before you finish, offer the person an opportunity to bring up anything not already dealt with. Ask for his or her comments on the process of the interview and share your own perceptions, making sure to acknowledge any positive contribution the person has made, e.g. the willingness to face difficult issues.

Exercise 8.28: Practising the Four 'Rs'

Group Structure: Individual then small group work.
Timing: 20 minutes.
Materials: Hand-out on the four 'R's.

Process: Ask people to think of someone whose behaviour they are not satisfied with at present, and to write down exactly what they would like to say to this person if they could speak freely.

When they have done this, invite them to rephrase what they have written into the four 'R' structure. A general discussion can ensue, focusing on difficulties and benefits of this kind of approach.

SUMMARY

We have make a brief tour through a range of managerial interventions, each designed to motivate individual members of staff and to deal with the kind of problems which can so easily hinder the progress of an organisation.

Realistically, of course, you will not be able to manage or solve all the problems with which you are faced. Organisations consist of a range of people with different needs, knowledge, skills and personalities. There are, for instance, the superstars who will always be achieving at a high level. There are those who, for a variety of reasons, constantly under-achieve, never really reaching their full potential. There are the rebels who seem intent on sabotaging your best efforts. Then there may be some who are just waiting to retire, giving the minimum . . . and so on.

However, if you can remain sensitive to the level of performance of each member of staff and plan your interventions in order to extend their effectiveness, even if only a little, you will increase your chances of creating a well-motivated staff group.

REFERENCES

Egan, G. (1975). *The Skilled Helper*. Brooks/Cole Publishing Co.
Handy, C. (1976). *Understanding Organisations*. Penguin.
Rogers, C. (1951). *Client Centred Therapy*. Houghton Mifflin.

STAYING HEALTHY

As we have seen, working in an organisation can be extremely stressful. There are times when the tension involved in balancing the needs of the organisation with each individual's needs can be overwhelming. So far we have explored how organisational structures and systems can contribute to the difficulties. We have looked at ways of changing these structures in order to reduce the problems for both the individual and the organisation. In this part of the book we approach the problem in a different way. Rather than focusing on what does or does not happen in the organisation, the core of this work is the person as an individual.

Like most things in life, there is good news and bad news about stress. One 'bad news' factor in that the physical and mental effects of too much stress often make themselves felt gradually so that the person, to a large extent, remains unaware of the physical and mental strain until the symptoms become really noticeable. By that time, the damage is sometimes serious and difficult to alleviate. But the good news is that it is possible to take control of one's reactions so that the stress is managed more effectively. The good news for trainers is that, assuming that people are motivated to want to change, the techniques which will help them are relatively easy to learn and teach. This part offers a range of such techniques covering breathing, self-massage and mental exercises, all of which are well-proven methods of stress reduction.

9

THE BREATH OF LIFE

This chapter takes as its focus something that we all do all the time, and, probably as a result of this, usually ignore. We are talking about breathing. One of the effects of stress is that we breathe inefficiently; as muscular tension increases, our breathing becomes more shallow. Many of us have been taught during our childhood to 'stand up straight', which usually means pushing your chest out and your belly in. This results in a posture which tightens the breathing muscles. In addition to this we can also unconsciously restrict our breathing as a way of suppressing painful emotions. Add to this the fact that many of us spend hours hunched over the computer, talking on the phone, sitting in uncomfortable chairs, rushing to meet deadlines—all of which affect those important muscles. Whatever the reason, many of us have fallen into habitually restricted breathing. This means our body and mind are not receiving the amount and quality of nourishment they need for peak performance. Encouraging people to learn and practise simple breathing exercises can greatly affect their feeling of well-being and their performance at work.

SESSION 21: BREATH OF LIFE

Training Objectives

1. To explain the importance of breathing and relaxation to general health and stress symptom reduction.
2. To teach exercises to improve breathing and relaxation.
3. To encourage development of practice sessions.

Notes for the Trainer

This session is presented at a very basic and practical level. It can serve as an introduction to the whole idea of taking more control over our physical self. If participants seem to be nervous or self-conscious about the exercises, start with those which are done by each person rather than pair activities. Working in pairs does have the advantage of immediate feedback as each person helps the other, but all of the exercises can be accomplished individually, so you may decide to run the entire session along those lines. A valuable by-product of these practice sessions is that they can be fun, and people very often report immediate beneficial effects like feeling more 'alive', more motivated, less tired and so on. This is a good session with which to end any course which has required people to concentrate hard for long periods, particularly if they have been fairly physically inactive.

Trainer Input

Breathing is something we all do all of the time, so you may be wondering why we are going to spend time learning about it. The way we breathe can affect our general outlook. Breathing well means our body is well nourished with the oxygen it needs to create energy; breathing poorly can make us feel tired and less able to meet the challenges of day-to-day living. Breathing is an unusual bodily function in that we can learn to control it consciously. By learning to deepen your breathing you can change the way you are thinking or feeling. If you are anxious or afraid, for instance, breathing can help you to calm yourself. Of all the ways of learning to control our stress, knowing how to breath well is simple, effective and cheap!

Before we continue, perhaps we should take a moment to explore why stress is such a problem. There is growing awareness of the toll that too much stress can take. There is a growing literature demonstrating the links between many illnesses and the stress of contemporary life. Living in a stressful world and working in a stressful organisation are bound to create tension. Of course, this is not altogether a bad thing for we all have a level of pressure which is right for us. It is only when this pressure is either higher or lower than this ideal level that we experience stress.

Exercise 9.1: The Stress Balloon

Group Structure: Individual work followed by group discussion.
Timing: Up to 15 minutes.
Materials: Each participant needs a sheet of blank paper and a pen.

Process: Tell the group that one way of perceiving stress is to think of a balloon. When a balloon is perfectly blown up there is a harmony between the pressure inside and outside its skin. Then ask them to imagine what will happen if more and more air is pumped into the balloon. Eventually the balloon bursts as the weakest point gives in to the pressure. On the

other hand, if you take most of the air out, all you get is a limp balloon—
not much good to anyone! Suggest that they draw themselves as that
balloon. The inside contains their inner selves: their hopes, fears, life
experiences, particular talents, personality traits and so on. Outside the
balloon are all the external pressures to which they are subject: the
demands of their job, people, the environment and so on. Ask them to
identify where they think the weak spots are: digestion, heart, back, mind,
etc. When they have their picture, give them a moment or two to think
about what they have drawn and then a general discussion can take place.

To understand why stress is a problem, we have to go back to pre-history. One
way of describing our problem is that we have developed minds capable of
creating travel to the moon and planets in bodies which are still living in caves.
Imagine yourself as one of your earliest ancestors. There you are, with your
family, sitting in your cave when you suddenly see the shadow of an enormous
monster on the cave wall. You look outside and see a dinosaur snuffling around,
obviously looking for its next meal. At this point you basically only have two
choices: you can run past the beast to get away to safety or you can stand and
fight. If you don't make up your mind quickly, you won't have a mind to make
up at all! The mechanism which developed to enable us to survive that kind of
trouble is still part of our make-up today. We call it 'fight or flight'.

Exercise 9.2: Stone Age in the Space Age: Stress Reactions

Group Structure: Small group work followed by discussion.
Timing: 15 minutes.
Materials: Flip chart sheets and pens for each group.

Process: Ask people to imagine themselves in the stress situations and to
list what they think their reactions would be under the headings of
Thoughts, Emotions, Physical Feeling and Behaviour. These can be
compared and discussed and will provide a general picture of stress
reactions.

SAMPLE SCENARIOS
1. You are in a heated argument with a senior colleague and something is
   said which indicates that he or she has completely misunderstood you.
2. You open a letter from your bank manager which tells you that you
   are severely overdrawn. As far as you know, you are well in credit.

As we can see, these situations trigger different responses; anger, frustration, fear, clenched fists, tense muscles, cold sweats, thoughts about running away and so on. The body is alerted by the brain to the potential threat (now not a dinosaur, but just as alarming to us in our modern life). This starts a chain of events which equips us to fight or flee. A variety of hormones are secreted, including adrenaline which increases the level of arousal in our body. Fuel has to reach the muscles which need to be strengthened for the coming activity. The bloodstream, the body's transport system, speeds up so your heart beats faster as the blood is pumped round more quickly than usual. The blood is directed away from the skin and internal organs and rushed to where it is most needed. We breathe more rapidly because the body needs more oxygen to burn its main fuel, glucose. The digestive system slows down because the body cannot cope with the normal process of digestion at the same time as all this other activity. You begin to sweat because the body needs to cool down the heat generated. All of this happens in a flash, and it is so familiar that we have given it various labels: fear, anxiety, panic, anger and so on. It is a problem because although it is a very effective way of dealing with life or death threats, it is not so good for the kind of threat any of us face in modern-day life. Most of the time, we cannot run away or strike someone. We have to contain our anger or fear and face the threat in some other way.

Good breathing helps to calm our body and mind so that we can intervene in what can become a very destructive cycle.

If you watch a young child or an animal you will see how their bodies move as they breathe. When you breathe freely, the diaphragm, belly and chest move with the rhythm of each breath, energising the whole body with oxygen. Sadly, as adults most of us have lost this knack and breathe shallowly without making full use of the diaphragm. Muscular tension, which could have evolved over years, is largely to blame for this shallow breathing. As we grow up many of us learn to control rather than express our deep feelings and this means tightening our breathing muscles and tensing our chests and abdomens.

To add to the problem, many of us have got into the habit of drooping over computer screens or writing desks, sitting in uncomfortable chairs at meetings, standing in crowded trains morning and evening—all of which tend to squash our lungs.

The exercises you will learn will help you free up your breathing so that, even when the heat is on and the tension high, you can be more in control of your responses. As you begin to breathe more easily, your body and mind are bound to benefit.

Exercise 9.3: Find Your Diaphragm

Group Structure: Individual work.
Timing: 10–15 minutes.

Materials: You need a room with space enough for people to lie on their backs on the floor. You may need to supply, or ask people in advance to bring, towels or mats to lie on.

Process: When people are comfortably settled on their backs on the floor, take them through the following set of movements:

Firstly, take a little time to become aware of how you are breathing now. This exercise is to show you how freely your chest and abdomen move when you breathe and will get you in touch with your diaphragm. Try breathing into your abdomen only, without moving your chest. You can imagine there is a ball just balanced on your chest and you have to breathe right down into your belly without moving the ball. Put your hands on your chest to check that it remains still. Continue like this until you are told what to do next. (*Stay quiet for two or three minutes.*) Next, breathe only into your chest feeling it rise and fall. This time put your hands on your belly to see that it does not move. (*Again wait for a few minutes.*) Which did you find easiest? Are you more comfortable breathing just into your chest or abdomen? Now put your arms down by your sides and breathe out. With your outbreath, bear down, puff out your belly and then release. Repeat a few times until you need to take another breath. (*Wait a few moments.*) Now reverse the movement, pulling in your abdomen and puffing out your chest after breathing out. Repeat just as before and then relax and breathe normally. If you combine these two movements, alternately puffing out the abdomen and then the chest, after breathing out you can feel your diaphragm moving just under your ribs. Relax for a while and then try it again. Notice how you are breathing as we finish the exercise.

After this breathing exercise, let us consider how we stand—our posture affects how we breathe. In fact, you could say that our posture reflects much about how we are experiencing life: holding back from it or facing it squarely; looking life straight in the eyes or bowing our heads before it. We are aiming for a stance which allows us to be flexible rather than static and stiff. This is explained by the following.

Exercise 9.4: Standing

Group Structure: Individual work in the group.
Timing: 10 minutes.

Process: After participants have found a space which allows them to swing their arms without hitting anyone, ask them to stand with their feet pelvis-width apart. Invite them to take off their shoes so that they can really feel their feet on the floor and take them through this exercise:

On the soles of your feet imagine a triangle between your heels and the joints beneath your big and little toes. Distribute your weight evenly on those triangles.

Now we are going to experiment with extremes for tension and relaxation so that you can find the best posture for yourself. Let yourself collapse in on yourself. Droop your head and shoulders and bend your knees. Notice how, as your shoulders come forward, your chest is restricted. *(Wait a minute or two to allow people to experience this way of standing.)* Now try standing with your knees locked, your shoulders thrown back and tense your lower back; keep your chin up. *(Again, wait a moment so people can feel the difference.)* Now find a mid-point between these positions. Start with your legs, relax your knees so that your legs feel ready for movement. Move your attention to your pelvis. Tilt it backwards as far as it will go then forwards and find a place between these two extremes. Move your attention to your head. Pull your chin right in to your throat and then push it forwards; now find the mid-point where your head sits naturally in line with your spine.

Now concentrate on your breathing; take in a slow breath to a count of 10, filling your lungs right down to your diaphragm. Hold it for a count of 10, then exhale fully also to a count of 10; hold it again for another count of 10 and start the cycle again.

Notes for the Trainer

You can give individuals feedback as you walk round the room; or suggest people work in pairs and help each other to find a good posture. A mirror or camcorder can be used to good effect so that people can see their own posture.

Trainer Input

Breathing is a very important part of relaxation. You might wonder why we need to learn to relax, but as we rush about from one part of our lives to another it is easy to forget how to let the tension go. To have various muscles constantly tense means we are wasting energy. Think about how many times a day you wrinkle your forehead, squint your eyes to see better, tap your fingers with impatience, shift about in your seat at a boring meeting, and so on. The trick to learn is how to use your energy when you need it and save it when you don't. During the breathing exercises you might have become aware of certain muscle groups being very tense. This exercise will help you locate these muscles and release them. This system is based on tensing and relaxing muscles in turn so that you can become more aware of the difference between tension and relaxation. We will go through the exercise and then discuss the practicalities of making this into a regular part of your self-care.

Notes for the Trainer

In the next exercise you will be taking participants through a progressive system of relaxation. It is worth while spending a little time in preparation; for instance, you need a warm, comfortable room in which you will not be disturbed. You may wish to turn the lights down to create a more relaxed atmosphere. As you talk through the exercise, keep your voice fairly soft and slow. Make sure you pause between each section to give people time to proceed at their own pace. There is nothing less relaxing than being rushed through a relaxation! It is suggested that people lie on the floor for this exercise and this is the best way to learn. However, if anyone in the group does not want to do this for any reason, he or she can follow the instruction sitting in a chair. You can suggest that people might be more comfortable if they take off their shoes and loosen any tight clothing in preparation. Those wearing glasses or contact lenses might be more comfortable without them.

Exercise 9.5: Relaxation

Group Structure: Individual work in the group.
Timing: 30 minutes.
Materials: Room for people to lie on the floor; you may need to ask participants to bring towels or mats to lie on.

Process: When people have found a comfortable place and are lying on their backs, take them through this relaxation exercise.

Take a moment to sense how you are at the moment without needing to do anything about it. Notice how your body feels and which thoughts come to you. Don't try to stop thinking, but just let the thoughts come and go without becoming too attached to anything particular. *(Pause.)*

Focus on breathing by putting one hand just below your rib cage and breathe in through your nose, taking the air to the bottom of your lungs so that your hand is pushed outwards. Fill your lungs right to the bottom, letting them expand. Hold for a few seconds. Now slowly breathe out through your mouth. When you reach the end of the breath, blow out just a little more so that you really empty your lungs. Repeat this a few times until you find a comfortable rhythm. (*Pause.*)

Now take another deep breath and tense every muscle in your body. Hold it briefly and then let it go as you breathe out. . . . Let your whole body relax; feel as if you are getting heavier and sinking into the floor as you become more relaxed. . . . Take another breath . . . hold the tension . . . let go as you breathe out. Notice how it feels to be tense and to be relaxed. (*Pause.*)

Keeping the rest of your body relaxed, wrinkle up your forehead . . . and let it go. Feel the tension slip away. Smooth out your forehead and take a deep breath. Squint up your eyes as if you were trying to see through a fog . . . now relax and let the tension around your eyes go. Open your mouth as wide as you can . . . feel the tension around your jaw and chin . . . now relax and let your mouth close. Let your tongue rest comfortably in your mouth and let your lips fall slightly apart.

Now shrug your shoulders right up to your ears and feel the tension in your shoulders and neck. Hold the tension . . . and relax and let go. Take a deep breath. Hold it. . . . Shrug your right shoulder up, feeling the tension along the right side of your neck. . . . Hold and . . . let go. Take a deep breath. Shrug your left shoulder and feel the tension along the left side of your neck. . . . Hold and . . . let go. Notice the difference in feeling tense and relaxed.

Stretch your arms out, making a fist of your hands. Hold the tension . . . and let go. Take a deep breath. Push your right hand down into the surface it is resting on . . . hold the tension in your hand and arm . . . and let go. Take a deep breath. Push your left hand down into the surface it is resting on . . . hold the tension in your hand and arm . . . and let go. Take a deep breath and slowly breathe out.

Bend your arms as if you were showing off your muscles . . . hold the tension . . . and relax. Take a deep breath . . . hold it . . . and let go, saying to yourself 'Relax and let go'.

Now concentrate on your chest . . . take a deep breath and as you hold it notice the tension. Say to yourself, 'Relax and let go' as you breathe out. Continue this way for a while . . . imagine your muscles relaxing with each breath.

Now imagine that you have a pillow under the middle and lower part of your back so you need to arch it up (or forward if you are sitting). Notice the tension and hold it for a while . . . say to yourself, 'Relax and let go' as you breathe out and let the relaxation spread into your back. Let's do a check now . . . head relaxed . . . neck relaxed . . . shoulders relaxed . . . chest relaxed . . . arms relaxed . . . back relaxed. . . . Imagine you are sinking into the floor or chair—a little more with each breath as you become more and more deeply relaxed. . . .

Focus on your abdomen . . . tighten up . . . and let go. . . . Push your abdomen out . . . hold for a moment . . . say to yourself, 'Relax and let go' and relax as you breathe out. . . . Pull your stomach in as far as you can . . . hold for a moment . . . say to yourself, 'Relax and let go' and breathe out.

Now we will move to your hips and legs. Press down your heels into the surface they are resting on . . . hold for a moment . . . relax and let go. . . . Curl your toes as if you were holding a pencil with them . . . hold . . . say to yourself, 'Relax and let go' and relax. Curl your toes upwards . . . hold . . . say to yourself, 'Relax and let go' and relax . . . wiggle your toes to free them of tension. Keep breathing slowly and deeply, feeling your body relax as you do.

Each time you breathe out, say to yourself, 'Relax and let go' . . . and check through your body, giving yourself instructions: face relax . . . shoulders relax . . . arms relax . . . hands relax . . . chest . . . back . . . abdomen . . . hips . . . legs . . . feet . . .

Concentrate on how it feels to be relaxed. If, during the day, you find yourself getting tense, take a breath and say to yourself, 'Relax and let go', remembering how it feels so that when you exhale you allow your muscles to loosen up.

When you are accustomed to using breathing to help you relax, you can get into the habit of focusing quickly on areas of particular tension and relaxing them.

Exercise 9.6: Tension Release

Timing: 5–10 minutes.

Process: Give participants time to get comfortable; they can be sitting on a chair or lying on their backs on the floor. When they are ready, take them through the following process:

If you feel tense anywhere, imagine that you can breathe into that tension as though you can actually exhale through that part of your body. Imagine your breath relaxing the sore muscle as it moves through it. As you breathe out, imagine the muscle letting go and letting the body loosen.

You can do this anywhere, anytime. If you are feeling tense or nervous, locate the tight place and breathe into it and then imagine breathing out the tension. In this way you are meeting the tension rather than resisting—and so reducing it.

Notes for the Trainer

There are many approaches to relaxation and you will be able to modify this particular suggestion to fit the time and the group you have. The main idea is to make it seem possible for people to do it fairly easily; people who are already stressed and busy won't take the time to do long relaxation sessions. The advantage of this approach is that, as people become familiar with the feeling of relaxation and the trigger words, they could learn to control their tension as and when it occurs. It is useful to begin or end each day of a course which has a self-care focus with such an exercise, because people do experience the benefits. Very often, participants report that they feel less tired at the end of the day or that they have been able to maintain their energy more effectively.

The next chapter takes this notion of self-care even further by introducing simple self-massage sequences which lessen tension and tiredness.

10

GIVE A BODY A BREAK

This chapter offers a way to teach simple exercises which can be done at any time, almost anywhere. They can be done with or without a partner and so are very appropriate for home or office. One of the sessions concentrates on preventing or reducing chronic pain. These sessions could be presented on their own or linked with those in Chapter 9 as a stress-reduction workshop. If you want to introduce this kind of practical stress control into other courses, individual sections can be included to start or finish the course work.

SESSION 22: CREATING ENERGY

Training Objectives

1. To explain how exercise can stimulate energy.
2. To present a series of simple five minute exercises.
3. To give practice time .

Trainer Input

We tend to think of stress as a totally bad thing, but another way of thinking about it is as too much of a very good thing. We need life to be exciting and stimulating otherwise we get bored and frustrated. What most of us could be better at is controlling our energy level, increasing or reducing it to meet whatever situation we are facing. The techniques we are going to learn and practise in this session enable you to do this when you need to relax but cannot take time out to do it. Most of them can be done very unobtrusively so you could use them while you were in the office or at a meeting if you cannot get away. They are aimed at stimulating circulation and easing tense muscles.

Notes for the Trainer

Each of these exercises is written as a 'script', taking you through the various exercises as you would instruct your participants. Where possible it is useful for you to demonstrate the exercises as you speak. Be sure to tell people to take part just to the extent of their comfort level; no prizes for being highest, quickest, or longest! The exercises are not intended as an athletics demonstration; they are meant to be enjoyable and relaxing. Emphasise that people should take responsibility in being careful with themselves.

Exercise 10.1: Energy for Face, Neck and Shoulders

Group Structure: Individual work in group with enough room for people to swing their arms around without hitting anyone.
Timing: Up to 10 minutes for each section.

Process: Find a space in the room to stand or sit. Many of the situations we find ourselves in at work can create tension in our face, neck and shoulders. Sitting over a VDU, facing an angry or upset member of the public, taking part in a difficult negotiation, getting out work to a tight deadline are all examples. These exercises will help you relax each part of your body.

Face: Place your fingertips lightly on your cheekbones and draw them gently and slowly down either side of your neck. Pull your fingers lightly across your collarbone and then sweep across the tops of your shoulders. You can use more pressure as you get to your shoulders. Imagine yourself collecting tension from your face and throwing it off your shoulders. Repeat this three or four times.

Now, again using your fingertips, place them on the centre of your forehead. Making tiny circles with your fingers, moving the skin beneath them so that the muscles are exercised, move them slowly to the ends of your forehead. Moving at your own pace, not too quickly, let your fingers travel all over your face, making these tiny circles. Areas like your cheeks, forehead, chin, jaw can take quite hard pressure; use a much lighter touch over your eyes and nose. If you come upon an area which feels tender, give it special attention. Think about relaxing and exercising the muscles of your face.

Jawbone: We often find ourselves having to clamp our mouths shut when we would rather speak or even scream. Think of the tension this creates for your jaws. To release some of this tension, place your thumbs on the corners of your jaw hinges just in front of the lobes of your ears and gently, but firmly, press into the jaw muscles. Slowly release the pressure and move to the next spot along your jaw bone. Work from the top down to the corners of your chin, pressing and releasing. Finish by letting your jaw fall open for a moment or two.

Releasing sinuses: If you find yourself suffering from painful sinuses—or headaches caused by blocked sinuses—this is a useful exercise. Place your middle fingers under your cheekbones to either side of your nose and again apply gentle but firm pressure. Press as deeply as is comfortable. Release the pressure gradually, and move along the bony ridges in this area pressing and releasing. Give extra attention to any particularly sensitive areas.

Notes for the Trainer

At this point you could stop and ask participants whether they notice any difference in how they are feeling. People often report feeling an immediate benefit from this kind of work, and you can point out that they have really spent very little time on it and did not need any lengthy instruction. These are things that can be done at any time and may be just enough to help someone over a particularly difficult situation or just get to the end of the day without feeling too tired.

Exercise 10.2 gives some more activities which also focus on the upper body.

Exercise 10.2: Releasing the Neck

Process: Feel the back of your neck with your fingertips. If you move your head slightly you will feel the ridge where the head is balanced on the spine. Tilt your head to the left, placing your middle finger in the groove just to the right of the base of the skull. Press up into this groove, slowly bringing your head upright and, moving your hand in towards the neck, press more deeply. Press and release gradually and then repeat on the left side. You can finish this exercise by applying light fingertip pressure to the front and sides of the neck, imagining that there are points down from neck, under the ears, to the top of the shoulder and pressing down on each one.

Release the shoulders: There is a very large, powerful muscle which stretches from the side of the neck out to the tip of the shoulders, draping onto the upper back. We can get very tense here and massage can release aches and pains. Squeeze gently along this muscle and then, using the middle finger, apply gradual pressure on any particularly tender spot to release tension. Work on both sides.

Release the head: Make your hands into fists, keeping the thumbs free. Tension can be released from the head by applying pressure with knuckles on the scalp just behind the temples and releasing. Another effective tension reliever is to rock the fists from index to little finger all over the scalp.

Stretch out: This group of exercises can finish with a good stretch. Clasp your hands behind your neck and lean back into them. Keeping the arms still, roll your head slowly from side to side using your clasped hands as a hammock, breathing in as you begin a turn to one side and out as you turn the other way.

Notes for the Trainer

The next group of exercises require participants to sit or lie on the floor. The exercises are aimed at helping to relax the back, legs and feet. When you come to the foot exercises, you may want to tell participants about the oriental theory of acupressure which relates different parts of the body to reflex points on the feet—reflexology. This is one way of explaining why a foot massage can be so relaxing and therapeutic. We start this section, though, with some activities to relax the back.

Exercise 10.3: Upper Back Release

Materials: For this series of exercises, participants will need floor space and a chair—preferably with a wooden back.

Process: Lie on your back on the floor and draw your knees up so they are pointing at the ceiling. Prop yourself up on your elbows so that your shoulders and head are lifted from the floor. Let your head relax backward. Relax your back and let your weight rest on your elbows. Release your neck muscles. When you feel the muscles relax, aim your chin towards each shoulder, rolling your head from side to side. Don't stretch beyond the point of comfort—you will notice that, as the muscles relax, your neck moves more easily. Gently lower yourself to the floor, breathing out and give yourself a stretch before you slowly sit up.

Exercise 10.4: Liberate your Middle Back

Process: You can stand or sit for this exercise, which is a simple stretch to loosen that hard-to-reach area of the middle back. Clasp your hands behind your head so that your elbows are spread back. You should be able to feel the stretch opening up your chest and take a breath. Lean to the right so that one elbow points to the floor and the other to the ceiling. Try not to bend forward as you do this—the idea is to keep the body upright to stretch out the ribs. Breathe out as you bring your head back to the centre; repeat the stretch to the other side.

Let yourself find your own rhythm and stretch from side to side keeping the movement smooth, breathing in as you stretch and out as you come back to the centre.

Exercise 10.5: Table Stretch

Materials: Chair and table for each participant, and some books to rest feet on to raise the level of knees to just above the hip joint.

Process: This is a particularly good activity if you spend a lot of time sitting writing or computing at a desk. Use the books to rest your feet on so that your knees are raised to just above the hip joint. Rest your head on your arms on the table. Close your eyes and breathe slowly and deeply for a minute or two. Feel the muscles in your back loosen as the pressure on the spine is lessened.

Trainer Input

We have focused on the top half of our bodies up to now, so let's bring our attention further down. Feet and legs are very important—they take our weight, move us along and in a more tangible way represent our connection with the earth. The oriental theory of reflexology adheres to the view that energy is constantly flowing through channels or zones in the body that terminate to form reflex points on hands and feet. When this energy flow is unimpeded we remain healthy, but when it is blocked by tension or congestion, disease occurs.

Exercise 10.6: Refresh your Feet

Materials: A small solid rubber or plastic ball for each participant.

Process: This is a series of foot exercises.

On the ball: Take a small ball and put it under the arch of your foot and roll it around, changing pressure as needed. Repeat on the other foot. If no balls are available, try the next exercise.

Foot rub: You need to take your shoes off for this. Start by rubbing the sole of one foot vigorously and carefully across the top of the other foot, moving from the heel to the arch to the toes. You can do this while sitting at a meeting or at one's desk and it does have a very refreshing effect.

Under the arches: In the reflex theory, the arch of the foot corresponds to the spine. Sit with your left foot on the right knee and, using your thumb, press along the side of the arch of the foot. Give any particularly sensitive spot some attention—pressing and releasing. Swap over and work on your right foot. This is another under-the-table activity!

Ankle press: Massage around your ankles, using the pressure-and-release system. Find the area under the ankle bone and press under the tiny tendon, lifting towards the bone. Using very light pressure to begin with, increasing as long as it is comfortable. Work on both ankles.

Groovy toes: Find the grooves between the bones of your foot and press your thumb into one of the grooves, running it slowly right up to the web between your toes. Work on each groove. Then place your fingertips on top of the foot and over the toes, gradually pulling your toes down to stretch out the foot. Now work on the other foot. A simple way of finishing with feet is to grasp the toes of one foot and gently fold your toes down as far as comfortable. Release the stretch gradually and then do the same with the other foot.

Trainer Input

Here are a group of stretching exercises which you can do while sitting in your chair—perhaps to give yourselves a break from desk work. As in all the exercises, only work to the extent of your comfort zone—you don't get a prize for over-straining your muscles and joints! The idea is to gently pull out the muscle fibres which have got scrunched up, rather like unravelling a skein of wool which has got tangled.

Exercise 10.7: Sit and Stretch

Process:
From the waist: Begin by sitting in your chair and take a couple of breaths. This exercise is a good way of relaxing those muscles that can get tensed up through sitting. Put one heel on top of the toes of the other foot and lean forward gently to touch your toes. Stay in this stretch for a while and move your attention through your body, releasing the neck so that the chin drops towards the chest, and releasing back muscles and straightening both legs as much as is comfortable. Lean from the waist and keep breathing deeply. Release the stretch slowly, sit upright, take a couple of breaths and repeat with the other foot on top.

Refreshing breath: This exercise is also done while sitting down and is very effective when you feel tired but you have to keep going. This breathing exercise is also a good way of giving yourself more energy. Sit upright with your palms on your lower abdomen. Concentrate on the out-breaths, exhaling fairly rapidly and deep, staying aware of your tummy muscles as you breathe out. You have to be careful with this exercise because it is possible to begin to feel light headed; if you do, take a few slow breaths and wait for your head to clear before beginning again. You can try this whenever you feel drowsy.

Breath and shrug: Another exercise you can do sitting or standing consists of breathing in and lifting both shoulders as high as possible. At this point you might notice just how tense you are. As you breathe out, let your shoulders drop. Find your own rhythm, aiming to make slow, smooth movements with muscles relaxing more with each cycle.

Everyone needs hugs: This is also a good releasing exercise for the upper back. Give yourself a hug by crossing your arms and clasping your shoulders, staying within the bounds of what is comfortable. Press your palms into your shoulders, pressing them away from the spine. Keep your spine straight and chin tucked under and feel your spine lengthening. Next turn from side to side by pivoting from your waist to left and right, keeping the movement slow and gentle.

You can modify this exercise by standing up and working on each shoulder in turn. Keeping one arm at your side, hold your shoulder with the other arm. Let your straight arm hang loosely and turn again from the waist, pulling your shoulder from right to left with the hand which is grasping the shoulder. As you turn the other way, let your shoulder and arm muscles relax. Before you repeat on the other side, notice any difference in your arms. One probably feels much more relaxed than the other!

Bend and stretch: This is another simple stretch that is good for those tense backs and can be done sitting down. Keep your spine straight and bend from the waist, leaning forward over your legs. Breathe out, releasing your back muscles, resting your chest as close to your thighs as is comfortable. Arms should drop down and neck and shoulders should be relaxed. Turn your head gently from side to side, breathing deeply and easily.

Trainer Input

Our hands also often get over-used and under-appreciated, so here are a set of exercises to relax and refresh them. Begin by spending a little time massaging each hand, giving each finger and thumb individual attention, pulling them out and massaging the joints. There is a reflexology theory linked to the hands as well as the feet, so a general massage is a way of paying attention to the whole body.

Exercise 10.8: Hand to Hand

Process: Participants can sit for this series of exercises. They are particularly pleasant if a little hand cream or oil is used.

Use your thumb and forefinger to gently massage the area from the base of the wrist down to the web between each finger.

Another way of massaging the hands is to interlock the fingers of each hand, making a 'basket' of the palms. The thumbs can then be used to massage the opposite palms, making sure of putting pressure between the bones. Now spread out the hand you have massaged. Use the fingers of your other hand to press upward behind your knuckles as you bend the fingers back as far as is comfortable. Now you can massage the areas at the base of each finger.

Now clench one hand and use it to massage the palm of the other. Slide your knuckles over the palm, pressing in between the bones.

Try making different sized circles—large and small. Switch hands.

Next, take each finger in turn and pull it out gently; try different speeds and experiment with spiralling your fist as you slide from base to tip of each finger—gently working the joints to keep them mobile.

Now grasp one wrist and move the skin in circles over the bones; work up the arm as far as possible and comfortable. Take the wrist and slide your clasped hand around it while you circle the wrist backwards and forwards.

End by shaking your hands loosely from the wrists.

SESSION 23: PREVENTING PAIN

Training Objectives

1. To provide exercises for specific areas of pain.
2. To demonstrate and practise these exercises.

Notes for the Trainer

Some people are suffering from chronic pain. Repetitive Strain Injury (RSI) is now a recognised medical condition and, as the name suggests, occurs as a result of constantly repeated muscle movements.

If you are providing training to have people lessen the effects of work strain on their bodies, you could consider including some of the following exercises which could be a preventative measure to help people avoid RSI, or at least relieve some of the pain. The exercises that follow are designed to alleviate specific areas of the body which are prone to pain when stressed. They are not so much to lessen pain which is already there as to prevent it occurring in the first place. As before, the exercises are described as a script which you can take people through. You could also use them as a hand-out so that, if it is inappropriate to include exercises in your training course, any participants who would be particularly helped can learn and practise the exercises.

Trainer Input

Headaches
Two sets of muscles in the forehead and temple area are responsible for many headaches. If this is a problem for you, try wrinkling your forehead into a frown. Notice the pull of the muscles across your forehead and the sides of your head. Hold this tense position for about 5 seconds and then relax. Be aware of the unwinding and relaxing muscles. Stay relaxed for about 3 seconds and then repeat.

Another exercise for these kind of headaches is to raise your eyebrow as high as possible, stretching your forehead and other muscles. Feel the tension, hold the position for about 5 seconds, and relax.

Don't worry too much if you find either of these exercises causing you more pain—it may actually be a good sign! It may mean you have identified the right muscle group to work on!

Stiff Upper Lip
Strange as it may seem, some headaches are actually caused by clenching your jaw muscles. In the struggle to remain calm and in control of a difficult situation, we might need to do a lot of this. If you think this might be contributing to your problems, this exercise may help:

Clench your teeth for 5 seconds, noticing the feeling of tension; now relax the muscle for about 30 seconds. If the muscles still feel tight, repeat.

Getting it in the Neck
A common culprit in the upper back, neck and shoulder area is the trapezius muscle which runs across the shoulders, up the neck and across the back of the head. You can suspect this muscle if you have neck or shoulder pain on occasion, especially if the pain begins in the neck or back of your head and radiates upwards. Tasks such as driving, word processing or any job which requires you to hold your hands in front of you can strain the trapezius

muscle, so check that your posture, the height of chair and angle of your monitor or workbench are right for you. These exercises should help you to monitor and control the amount of muscle tension you experience.

1. To tense your neck area, bring your head forward until your chin almost touches your chest. Now prevent it from doing so by pretending that there is a force pushing it away from your chest and struggle against this force. You should feel that you are lifting your head, but not actually moving it. Keep the tension for about 5 seconds and then return to normal. Wait for a couple of seconds for muscles to fully relax and notice any difference in feeling. Let the relaxation continue for about 30 seconds. If you do not feel fully relaxed, repeat once again.
2. Push your head backwards as far as is comfortable. Tense your neck and hold for about 5 seconds. Relax and return your head to its normal position. Rest for about 30 seconds and repeat once again if you do not feel fully relaxed.
3. Pull your shoulders towards each other behind your back. Hold for about 5 seconds and relax. Rest for about 30 seconds, and repeat once more if you wish.
4. Hunch up until your shoulders touch your ears. Keep this up for about 5 seconds and then relax. Rest for about 30 seconds and repeat once again if you wish.

The point behind all these exercises is for you to be more aware of the difference between tension and the relaxed state and to be able to move from one to the other at will. Using this kind of technique will help you to be much more in control of just how tense you become.

Notes for the Trainer

How much of this kind of work you introduce into a training course obviously depends on your training objectives. If you would like to include more simple stress-reducing massage, the reference section lists several books that will help you understand the benefits.

The next chapter continues the theme of taking steps to remain as healthy as possible in what may be a stressful environment by focusing on simple and relaxing meditation techniques.

REFERENCES

Chia, Mantak (1986). *Chi Self-Massage*. New York: Healing Tao Books.
Kent, Anne (1994). *The Modern Book of Massage*. Aquarian/Harper Collins.
Lidell, L. (1990). *The Book of Massage*. Ebury Press.
Peck, Connie (1982). *Controlling Chronic Pain*. Fontana

11

USE YOUR MIND

In this chapter we are building on the idea of encouraging people to take some action in managing themselves physically and mentally so that they are not so much at the mercy of the stresses and tensions that seem to absorb a large part of modern organisational life. We will look at the potential of meditation and visualisation as a method of relaxing or dealing with anxiety.

Notes for the Trainer

If you choose to include some of this work in your training programme it would be useful to know whether your training group are familiar with these techniques. If they are not, you will need to provide some preparation—perhaps simple, short exercises together with an explanation of how meditation works. Sometimes people have a very hazy idea of what it involves, believing they would have to adopt special (and uncomfortable) positions for a very long time. They might assume that you need to belong to a particular religious group or cult. In fact, none of this is really true. Meditation and visualisation are often used together with relaxation, and have a good effect for calming down anxiety or preparing for action. Meditation is the discipline of relaxing your mind in order to focus your energy. There is not really a right way to do it; there are many approaches and people usually adopt a system with which they feel comfortable.

This chapter starts with a set of introductory inputs and exercises, and continues with suggestions for ways to put them to practical use.

SESSION 24: INTRODUCTION TO MEDITATION

Training Objectives

1. To explain the purpose and practice of meditation and visualisation.
2. To provide introductory demonstration exercises.
3. To explore how meditation can be practised regularly and in everyday situations.

Trainer Input

This session is about using your mind to help you keep calm and in control. We will be exploring techniques of meditation and visualisation which you will have an opportunity to try out for yourself. Meditation is a wonderful way to quiet the mind and focus your mental energy. You may have heard about different techniques, some of which involve sitting in uncomfortable positions for a long time, or making special sounds, or are attached to some esoteric ritual. In fact you do not have to do anything other than arrange a time and place where you can be comfortable and undisturbed. Let's try this Exercise.

Exercise 11.1: Simple Meditation

Group Structure: Whole group followed by discussion.
Timing: 5–10 minutes.

Process: When you have made sure that everyone has some space either sitting or lying down, take people through this exercise: 'Shut your eyes and be aware of your breathing. Feel your breath coming into your lungs and feel it going out. Be aware of your chest and abdomen as you breathe. Don't pay attention to anything else but your breath. As you hear sounds or notice thoughts come into your head or become aware of physical sensation or discomfort, just note them and let them go. Go back to your concentration on your breathing.'

When you have finished, ask the group to open their eyes and reflect for a moment on their experience. The kind of questions you can ask include 'Did you have any problems doing this?', 'Did you find yourself thinking uninvited thoughts?', 'Did you find yourself forgetting how to breathe because you were concentrating so hard?', 'Did five minutes seem a long time?'.

Trainer Input

People often ask why meditation is useful; after all, it just seems like sitting and doing nothing and can seem very self-indulgent and even lazy. Although you might just have had a taste of the work involved in meditation, you weren't really sitting doing nothing—you were actively attempting to control your mind.

The practice of meditation can reduce tension and promote relaxation. By meditating regularly you can improve your ability to concentrate and decrease anxiety symptoms. We are learning much more about the relationship between the mind and body. Increasingly we are understanding that our thoughts affect our feelings and they both affect our health.

If you were a musician or an athlete you would not question the importance of practising your scales or strengthening those muscles which help you to run. Your mind is one of your main resources to help you do your job and, more than that, to live your life as fully as possible. Meditation offers a way to develop strength and clarity of mind. The following exercises show you different ways of approaching meditation.

Exercise 11.2: Meditation Practice

Group Structure: As for simple meditation.
Timing: 5 minutes for each exercise; followed by discussion.

Process: As in the previous exercise, start by ensuring that everyone has space and is comfortable; if the room has very bright lights, you might switch some of them off to provide a more restful atmosphere. Take people through each exercise and then give time for discussion or questions. It is important to make the point that there is no 'right' way to do meditation; it is a very personal experience and everyone finds his or her own way. These exercises are to provide examples of possible approaches to give people a taste of the experience.

USING AN IMAGE
Take one or two deep breaths and close your eyes. Think of a simple design like a circle or a cross. Any symbol which means something to you and is easy to visualise will do. Keep it simple, though. Now keep that design in your mind; if you find your mind wandering, do not blame yourself—you are not doing anything wrong. Just gently bring your mind back to the image you have chosen.

USING AN OBJECT
Sometimes people find it hard to conjure up an image in their mind, so here is a way to meditate using some external object. Rest your hand gently in front of you so you can look down at your thumbnail. Keep looking at your thumbnail—you do not have to strain your eyes; keep them relaxed. Be aware of your breathing and keep looking at your thumbnail. You do not have to think any deep thoughts about it, just keep your eyes focused. Again, if you find your mind wandering, gently bring it back to the task in hand.

This exercise can be done with any object: a vase, a flower, a candle; anything that is meaningful to you and easy to set up.

COUNTING BREATHS

If you find it hard to concentrate on an image or an object, you might be more comfortable with a sound. Relax and close your eyes; now begin to count your breaths—each inhalation and exhalation counts as one breath. Say the words 'one', 'two', etc., to yourself in your mind. Work up to ten, then start again. If you lose count, don't worry—just start again.

THOUGHT BUBBLES

There is a myth that meditation means not thinking. As you can see, it doesn't really mean this at all. This exercise is based on the thoughts which will naturally arise. Once again close your eyes and relax. Don't do anything in particular. Allow thoughts to come into your head and then to fade away. Imagine that you put each thought into a bubble and then watch that bubble float away in your mind's eye.

When the practice time is up for this exercise you can ask participants to review their thoughts; perhaps there will be an insight into a particular situation or a deeper awareness of some aspect of life. Sometimes people discover that much of their thinking is taken up with going over the past or wondering about the future; this can lead them to an awareness of how much they may be ignoring their present experience.

FOCUSING ON A COLOUR

Once again sit and relax. Now choose a colour; start with something from the cool range—blue, green, violet. Fill your mind with this colour as you practise; as before, if you find your mind wandering from the task in hand, gently bring it back to the colour you have chosen.

If you wish to develop this exercise you can suggest that people choose a colour from the 'hot' range—red, orange or yellow—and notice the way that different colours can affect our system or mood.

Trainer Input

One of the purposes of this session is to explore how you can use meditation in your everyday life to help you reduce stress and improve your mental and physical state. Let us spend a little time considering this.

Exercise 11.3: Making Meditation Practical

Group Structure: Group discussion.

Timing: Up to 20 minutes.

Process: This exercise could start with a brainstorm; people giving ideas as to when and where they could meditate if they decided to make this part of their general health plan. Examples could include:

When:

- Beginning or end of each day
- On return from work
- At regular intervals during the day
- Just before stressful event
- During boring meetings
- During journey to work (not if you're driving!)

Where:

- Private space
- Bedroom
- Bathroom
- Walk in the park
- In the office if it's possible to be undisturbed
- Garden

This can be followed by a discussion about the pros and cons of using this way of calming or preparing oneself for whatever is happening. As you take part in the discussion you might point out the advantage that it doesn't cost anything and doesn't need equipment or a special place—only some undisturbed time.

Trainer Input

Jessica Macbeth (1990) gives some very helpful practical advice for people who want to make meditation part of their overall health care programme. She suggests creating a short, simple ritual to allow our body and mind to shift into a meditative state—like changing gear. Obviously this needs to be done with common sense—there is no point in making up an elaborate ceremony which requires all sorts of symbolic objects. All that happens is that the ceremony takes over; what is important is that you find a little time to spend on resting and energising your mind—you do not want to exhaust it with complicated ceremonial. It can be as simple as a particular phrase—for instance, 'Now, I'll be peaceful'—or two or three deep breaths. In working out your own ritual, keep it simple, internal, easy to remember and gentle. Be clear about what you want the ritual to do for you. The obvious purpose is to change mental and physical gear; however, you might feel you need some protection from your environment, in which case you could visualise yourself surrounded by white light which shelters and protects you. You can also think about a ritual for finishing the meditation and returning to your everyday world. Again, a phrase and a couple of breaths could work very well.

Exercise 11.4: Preparation for Meditation

Group Structure: Individual work followed by general discussion.
Timing: 15 minutes.

Process: At this point, you could suggest that participants may want to think about a ritual that would work for them. A general discussion could follow with people sharing their ideas.

Another practical matter is how to stay awake. One of the problems which many people encounter, particularly as they begin this practice, is falling asleep. It is hardly surprising, especially after a day's work. Jessica Macbeth suggests sitting in a comfortable chair with arms on which you can rest your elbows. When you are comfortable, raise one forearm vertically in the air. In this position you can keep your forearm raised as long as you stay awake. If you begin to nod off, your arm will drop and wake you up. This is why meditating while lying in bed is not a good idea—unless you want to increase your sleep quota.

SESSION 25: CREATIVE VISUALISATION

Training Objectives

1. To build on the previous session by introducing visualisation.
2. To demonstrate different techniques.
3. To discuss participants' experiences of the exercises.

Notes for the Trainer

You can develop this work by introducing people to the idea of creative visualisation. Shakti Gawain (1982) suggests that thought is a quick, light, mobile form of energy which manifests instantaneously. When we create something, we always create it in thought form. A thought or idea always precedes manifestation. 'I think I'll make stew for dinner', 'I want a new job', 'I'll paint that scene' are all examples of thoughts which precede action. The idea is like a blueprint; it creates an image of the form which guides the action.

If your group is receptive to this idea you can demonstrate how visualisations can be used to guide thinking and energy. Probably the most important thing is, as in the previous session, to allow people to air their ideas about this kind of activity with the aim of dispelling anxieties about the sense of mystery and strangeness that can surround it. Many people have already experienced the power of thought; how when we feel negative, fearful or insecure we often seem to attract the very experiences we are trying to avoid. In contrast, if our attitude is positive, we seem to have the energy to manage or control situations so that they conform more to our expectation of success or happiness. A discussion with people sharing their experience in relation to this idea can be useful at this point.

Trainer Input

It isn't that 'positive thinking' can change us or our lives in a magic way. This process of thinking more deeply involves exploring and perhaps changing our basic attitudes to life. We can use our mind to help us understand how we might be holding ourselves back from achieving satisfaction; creating barriers which prevent us from moving on in our lives. Very often as we relax and let images develop in our mind, those images become a window into our self, showing us things which are usually hidden by the everyday activity with which our lives are filled.

There is no right way to visualise, so do not allow yourself to get trapped into anxieties about 'doing it right'. Some people see very clear pictures when they imagine something; others feel they just think about it rather than actually see something; others experience feelings which seem to emerge. All of these reactions are fine; let's just go through a few practice exercises and see what happens.

Exercise 11.5: Simple Visualisation

Group Structure: Participants need to be sitting comfortably in a fairly warm room. It can be helpful to turn the lights down.
Timing: 10 minutes.

Process: When you have made sure that people are comfortable, begin. Close your eyes and breathe deeply; let yourself relax. Think of a room that you like to be in; a comfortable room at home or maybe somewhere else. Remember as many details as you can; the colour of the walls, the texture of the carpet, tables and chairs. Build up the picture in your mind, and as you remember each item place it in your mental picture. *(Stay silent for a while, so people have time to focus their thoughts.)* Now imagine yourself walking into the room and making yourself comfortable. Perhaps you sit in a particular chair or lie on a couch or the floor. Let yourself enjoy the feeling of security and comfort. *(Wait a short time before continuing.)*

Now call to mind a pleasant experience—a delicious meal, a meeting with a dear friend, being praised for work well done, anything that made you feel really good about yourself and the world in general. Recall the experience and try to recreate the feelings that went with it. Once again, allow yourself to enjoy those feelings. *(Wait a few seconds before continuing.)*

Now visualise a pleasant outdoor place which you have visited, or would like to visit if it existed. Make the picture of it in your mind: it could be in the mountains, or beside a river, in a forest; it could be desert or rainforest; a garden or park. Just somewhere you would love to be. Create the details in your mind; the climate, the time of day. *(Again, wait a few seconds.)*

Now take a couple of deep breaths and think about returning to this room. When you feel ready, open your eyes and give yourself a good stretch.

*   *   *

If this is the first time participants have experienced this kind of exercise, give some time for discussion.

Notes for the Trainer

You may find that some people are convinced they cannot do this kind of thing or are too self-conscious to allow themselves to relax into it. It is important not to put pressure on them; reassure them that however they do the exercise is acceptable. If they do not want to take part, suggest they stay with their own thoughts during the exercise. They can share these with the others if they wish or keep them to themselves. Very often, the fear of 'not doing it right' or appearing silly before others is at the root of reluctance. As the group continues to work with the exercises, people can begin to see the insight and enjoyment to be had and will join in at their own pace.

What follows are a series of visualisation 'scripts' which you can adapt to your own objectives if you wish to develop this kind of course.

Exercise 11.6: Visualisation: Stay with the Pain

Purpose: This exercise provides a different way of responding to pain. Very often our natural reaction is to resist or ignore it, but this can make us very tense and the tension can increase the pain we feel. This exercise can release that tension and at times effectively reduce the pain.

EXERCISE

Sit comfortably, close your eyes and concentrate for a while on your breathing. Let your breath flow freely and deeply.

Allow your attention to go to the area of pain. Don't do anything with the pain, just rest your awareness on the surrounding area. Imagine yourself breathing into the centre of the pain and that each breath warms and softens that area. As you continue to breathe, give your breath a colour or texture so that you create an image in your mind of the painful area being surrounded by your breath. Continue to do this until you feel this area has become as warm and as soft as possible.

If you lose your concentration, don't worry. Just return to the idea of your warm breath and the image you are creating.

As you continue, allow the effect of your relaxation gradually into the rest of your body, letting any tension go. If the pain claims your attention again, return to that area and acknowledge it.

Imagine the warmth and softness of your breath radiating throughout your body; to the tips of your fingers and toes and the top of your head. Take your time and imagine each part of your body clearly.

Now take a couple of deep breaths, open your eyes, give yourself a good stretch and try to keep the feeling of calm and softness with you.

Exercise 11.7: Visualisation: On the Island

Purpose: Relaxation.

EXERCISE

Sit comfortably; close your eyes and breathe slowly and deeply. Picture yourself on a mountaintop, above a tropical island. It has just finished raining, the sun is shining, the sky is clear and blue. Below you can see the bright green of the trees, raindrops glistening on the leaves, reflecting the sun. You can see the bright colours of the flowers—red, yellow, blue, orange. You can hear the slap of the sea against the beach which you can see beyond the trees. The sand is golden and you can see palm trees all along the beach.

You look farther—out to sea—where the water is clear as crystal. Enjoy the feeling of being on the top of the mountain, and when you are ready take a couple of deep breaths and return to wherever you are in the present. Open your eyes and let yourself stretch. Take the feeling of peace and relaxation into your next activity.

Exercise 11.8: Visualisation: In the Boat

Purpose: Preparation for dealing with potential stressful situation.

EXERCISE

Sit comfortably, close your eyes and concentrate on your breathing for a short while.

Picture yourself on the grassy bank of a river. Take some time to look around you; listen to the birdsong, feel a gentle, warm breeze; notice the wild flowers growing though the grass.

You can hear the water lapping along the river bank and you see a small boat tied up. Imagine yourself stepping into the boat. In the bottom of the boat are cushions which you arrange to make yourself comfortable. Untie the boat and let yourself float in the river. The boat rocks gently from the motion of the water as you drift down the river.

You lie back in the boat, watching the clouds move slowly past; listening to the water gently slapping the boat; you feel peaceful and calm.

Very gradually the boat picks up speed and you get the sense of moving towards a destination. You enjoy the feeling of purpose as the boat gently floats to the bank. When you feel ready, you step out of the boat and tie it up—so that it is ready to carry you when you need it.

Stand on the bank for a moment, breathe in the fresh air of the countryside, take a look at the boat which has brought you here and slowly turn round and begin to walk away—towards your next objective. Take a couple of deep breaths, open your eyes and stretch.

This is the end of Part III, which has suggested ways of introducing people to techniques for reducing stress that may be affecting them and thereby helping them to remain healthy.

Part IV will explore possibilities for using training to help people to move on in their organisation or their career or who are facing retirement or redundancy.

REFERENCES

Gawain, S. (1982). *Creative Visualization*. Bantam New Age Books.
Macbeth, J. (1990). *Moon Over Water*. Bath: Gateway Books.

INTO THE FUTURE

So far we have concentrated on how to use training to help people stay working in their organisations as effectively, as healthily and as happily as possible. However, there are times when people need to consider a change. Perhaps they want to move on in their organisation or progress in their career, or they may be facing redundancy or retirement. The first chapter of this part suggests training structures which help people assess their progress so far and clarify how they want or need to develop. The next chapter focuses on decision making for future development and, finally, issues relating specifically to redundancy and retirement will be explored.

12

WHERE ARE YOU NOW?

In organisations which offer personal development training, there is often a call for help in career progress. These first sessions provide useful structures within which individuals can assess their skills and experience and identify possible developmental options. They can stand on their own as a training workshop for people wanting to explore possibilities of developing themselves, or as an introduction to a course for people who are preparing for retirement or facing redundancy. You will be able to tailor your input to match the particular needs of the group.

SESSION 26: CAREER LIFE PLANNING

Training Objectives

1. To identify relevant experience, personal resources and skills.
2. To clarify hopes and ambitions for development.
3. To describe potential barriers to achievement.
4. To identify career options.

Notes for the Trainer

You will see from the first exercise that this workshop is focused around people's perception of the resources they bring to any job. They are encouraged to see their life experience as an important source, to be considered along with academic qualifications or vocational training. There is also a 'hidden agenda' to this exercise, which is to increase people's confidence, particularly if they are thinking of applying for new jobs.

It is a great boost to self-esteem to realise that one is a unique and valuable person as a result of one's life experiences as well as more obvious qualifications. Feeling stuck in an unsatisfying job or searching for employment can create feelings of despondency, low self-esteem or even hopelessness. These feelings can create a descending spiral perhaps leading to despair which, in turn, makes it hard for the person to generate the energy necessary to make the needed or desired changes. The following sessions, if successful, should leave people feeling more hopeful and ready to take the necessary action.

Exercise 12.1: Life-Line

Group Structure: Individual work followed by discussion in pairs or small groups.
Timing: Up to one hour.
Materials: 2 × A2 or A3 sheets of paper for each participant; coloured pens.

Process: The exercise should be performed in two parts.

Part 1: Give all the participants a blank sheet of paper and ask them to take some coloured pens. Ask them to take one sheet of paper and draw a line like this:

B ——————————————————————————— D

Explain that 'B' stands for the day of their birth and 'D' for the day of their death. Ask each person to place a X to indicate where they think they are now. Having done that, suggest they look at it for a few minutes. Ask them to ask themselves: 'What do you think and feel about the point you have reached?', 'What do you want to achieve in the time that's left?', 'How would you feel if you reached D-day with nothing having changed?', 'What do you feel about the time you have spent so far?'

This might lead to a group discussion or you might suggest that the group split into pairs to discuss thoughts and feelings which have arisen in a more personal way.

Part 2: Now hand out another sheet of paper and ask people to place a mark in the top left-hand corner. This mark represents their birth; ask them to draw a line from that mark which could represent their life up to the present moment. They should mark any milestones from which they feel they have learned something. Point out that learning to walk and talk were probably the most important learning milestones of their entire career—and make it clear that you are thinking of more than the obvious academic or vocational successes.

You can also suggest that people can be as creative as they want in their representation; some might see their life as a journey with various stops on the way; others as a map, or a 'snakes and ladders' game—or whatever. The point is that people should enjoy this rather than see it just as a memory exercise.

You can also point out that milestones can be pleasant or painful but each experience is an opportunity for learning and developing strengths and resources. For instance, a woman who has brought up children will have developed many skills which she might think are irrelevant to her work. A man who has tended an aged parent might similarly believe that he has learned nothing of use from the experience.

When people have finished, ask them to look at the picture they have made and to list the knowledge or skills they could have gained from each milestone. These are the resources which are available to help them make the changes they want.

The final stage of this exercise is for people to talk about the resulting thoughts and feelings so that they can make an informed assessment of their present situation; their strengths and weaknesses, qualities which can help or hinder them in their future movement.

Trainer Input

Have you ever played the game, 'If only I could/had/hadn't/was/wasn't . . .'? You know, 'If only I'd gone to University'; 'If only I'd taking studying more seriously'; 'If only I'd changed jobs'; 'If only I was better at English'; 'If only I wasn't so timid' . . . We all have our own list. This workshop gives you the opportunity to think beyond this game. Our next exercise, moving on from the previous one, will help you clarify what you want and need for the future.

To do this you need to build up your confidence in your sense of control over yourself and your life. This means knowing that you

- are open to change
- have the skills to change
- recognise the gap between where you are now and where you want to be
- can clarify the action steps which will take you where you want to be
- are willing to act on the action plans . . . and
- are aware of the possible need to change those plans if necessary.

Exercise 12.2: Building Blocks

Group Structure: As before, personal work followed by small or large group discussion.

Timing: Up to one hour.
Materials: Paper and writing implements for each person.

Process: Start by suggesting the idea that we each need a number of building blocks for change which can be categorised as:

- Values. (What is important to me in my life?)
- Goals. (What do I want to achieve?)
- Beliefs. (What beliefs do I hold which will help or hinder me in getting what I want?)
- Knowledge. (What do I need to know to get what I'm aiming for?)
- Skills. (What skills do I need to get what I want?)

Give people time to think about and write down their answers to the questions. Then suggest that they draw their own 'brick wall' with a brick for each point they have identified.

When the 'walls' have been drawn, people can discuss them in pairs or small groups.

Trainer Input

You have identified some of the building blocks you can use to help you with the changes you want to make. These are the elements for which to aim if you want to exert some control over how your life is going, rather than just reacting to whatever is happening at the moment. The next exercise contains some more questions to help you begin to make your plans.

Exercise 12.3: Six Questions for a Plan

Group Structure: Individual questionnaire followed by discussion.
Timing: 40 minutes.
Materials: One copy of the questionnaire for each participant.

Process: Give out the questionnaire and give people time to complete it. Its purpose is to show the process of career and life management and provide a logical process of thinking the issues through.

SIX QUESTIONS FOR CAREER AND LIFE MANAGEMENT
Answering these questions will enable you to begin to plan for the next phase of your career.

1. *Who am I?* (What are my transferable skills, my values, my interests?)

2. *Where am I now?* (Which stage of life am I at? What kind of career pattern do I want? Where am I in that pattern?)

3. *How satisfied am I?* (What are the roles I occupy; e.g. parent, employee, friend, consumer, artist, gardener, home-maker, partner, etc.? How much do each of these roles satisfy my expectations?)

4. *What changes do I want?* (The answer to this question can, of course, be 'none'. However, it is still a useful exercise to review your life up to now. You may find that things are going exactly as you planned and want. If not, you have a chance to identify and clarify the changes which would make your life more as you would like it.)

5. *How can I make sure these changes happen?* (Once you have identified the changes you want, the next step is to construct an action plan capable of achieving the objectives. You can also think about people who might support you through the changes and resources that might make it easier for you to succeed.)

6. *What will I do if it doesn't work out?* (It is always good to have a plan to fall back on if you don't succeed in your schemes. It is so easy to feel that if a particular plan of action fails, you have failed as a person. But it isn't YOU that has failed—just your objectives. Perhaps they were not realistic or adequate, or perhaps external events that you couldn't have forecast influenced the outcome. So work out what you will do should this happen.)

Trainer Input

Having just answered six questions, let us now consider seven skills. These are the skills that will help you most in the preparation and execution of your future plans.

1. *Self-knowledge:* There are many aspects of yourself that you can call upon to help you, but in order to do that you need to know what they are. Some of the work we have done so far will have enabled you to build up a picture of your talents and qualities, your strengths and weaknesses.

Exercise 12.4: What Do You Look Like?

Group Structure: Individual work followed by general discussion.
Timing: 15 minutes.
Materials: Blank sheet of paper and coloured pens for each person.

Process: Ask participants to draw a large outline of a person on their sheet of paper (If you think people will get put off by having to draw, you could supply sheets with the outline already drawn.) Suggest that they add words or phrases to mark their own particular talents, qualities, strengths, weaknesses, etc. (e.g. 'a good listening ear', 'strong shoulders', 'big heart', and so on).

Then ask people to move into pairs or small groups and, using their drawings as a trigger, help each other build up a realistic list of personal resources.

---

2. *Learning from experience:* Have you noticed how some people never seem to learn from their mistakes, but just keep repeating them over and over?

Exercise 12.5: Learn from Experience

Group Structure: Individual work.
Timing: 15 minutes.

Process: Ask participants to remember a recent event which did not work out the way they expected or wanted. Ask them to jot down their answers to these questions:

- What happened?
- What can I learn from it?
- As a result, what will I do again/not do again?

---

3. *Research:* This means knowing how to access the information you may need to help you.

Exercise 12.6: Resources Brainstorm

Group Structure: Whole group.
Timing: 5 minutes.

Process: Using a flip chart, organise a brainstorm asking people to call out any possible people, places or objects that could be resources to help them.

---

4. *Defining aims; setting objectives; making action plans:* One of the reasons people do not get what they want in life is because they have never worked out exactly what they do want. They may be feeling dissatisfied, that

something is not right but they have never really developed the skill of converting complaints into aims, aims into objectives and objectives into action plans.

- An *Aim* is a general statement of what you want to happen, e.g. 'I want to get promotion'.
- An *Objective* is much more specific, e.g. 'I want to become a district manager'.
- An *Action Plan* describes the steps that need to be taken to achieve the objective.

Exercise 12.7: Aims, Objectives and Action Plans

Group Structure: Small group work.
Timing: 20 minutes.
Materials: Brief case studies for each group

Process: Provide each group with a set of statements and ask them to convert them into aims, objectives and action plans.

Examples might include: 'I want to get a new job'; 'It would be good to have more leisure time'; 'No one seems to want to co-operate with me'; 'My life just seems empty at the moment.'

---

5. *Decision making:* You have to be careful that you do not collect so much information that you confuse yourself and cannot decide what to do. Decision making requires the ability to generate alternative choices based on good information and being able to decide between them. Here is a chance to explore one way of making a decision.

Exercise 12.8: Pros and Cons

Group Structure: Small groups.
Timing: 20 minutes.

Process: Ask each group to choose an example of a decision-making situation; e.g. The choice between full- and part-time work; what career pattern do I want? They should list all the pros and cons of each choice. The next step is to rank each item in terms of importance and then discuss the decision which the results of the exercise might suggest.

---

6. *Caring for yourself:* None of this is particularly easy. Change always involves some level of stress—even change for the better. Knowing how to look after yourself physically, mentally, emotionally and spiritually is as important as any of the other skills we have discussed.

Exercise 12.9: Looking After Yourself

Group Structure: Whole group.
Timing: 10 minutes.

Process: A brainstorm, asking participants to offer any suggestions for ways of maintaining good physical and mental health.

---

7. *Communication:* Career and life management is a mixture of thinking and working by yourself and contact with other people. There are bound to be times when you might want to seek advice or help; explain what you want to do; ask for support or communicate with others for some other purpose. You need to be capable of expressing yourself clearly, in speech and in writing.

Exercise 12.10: Talking About It

Group Structure: Pairs.
Timing: 15 minutes.

Process: Instruct participants to sit together in pairs, facing each other and spread around the room so that they can talk to each other without feeling too close to other pairs. Explain that this is an exercise in putting thoughts and feelings into words rather than having a discussion, so that while one person is talking the other will listen in an encouraging way. Emphasise that it is not necessary to talk about anything which needs to be kept confidential—this is not an exercise in baring your soul! On the other hand, you can remind people that, as fellow course participants, they have a general obligation not to gossip about each other outside the course.

In the first part of the exercise, ask the first person to talk to the second about their career hopes for the future for five minutes.

In the second part, the roles will switch and the second person will talk to the first about any fears they may have with regard to their career plans—again for five minutes.

> The last part of the exercise will take place in the whole group, where people can talk about their experience of the exercise.

Trainer Input

So far in this session we have concentrated on identifying the kinds of changes or progress you may be wanting to make and, by now, you should be much clearer about your hopes and expectations. Life, as you probably know by now, is not always co-operative and there are probably going to be some barriers to success. Let's spend a little time considering what these might be.

Exercise 12.11: Barriers Brainstorm

Timing: 15 minutes.

Process: Ask participants to call out anything at all which they feel could present a barrier to their success. Encourage people to include what they may think are trivial details as well as the obvious things. For example: personality traits, other people's reactions, lack of resources, inability to sustain motivation, other demands and so on. List everything on a flip chart.

When the list is complete, give some time for a general discussion and then suggest that people jot down those items which they feel particularly relate to them.

Notes for the Trainer

This may be all you wish to do with regard to barriers and there is certainly a case to be made for not focusing too long on problems in case people begin to feel daunted by what they may face. If, however, you want to spend some more time on clarifying the nature of the possible barriers, you can offer the following exercises.

Exercise 12.12: Facing the Problems

Group Structure: Whole group activity and discussion.
Timing: 20 minutes.

Process: Give out small oblong pieces of paper (shaped like bricks) and ask people to write anything they think might be a barrier to change—one item per brick. Then suggest that people put their bricks on the floor, building up a wall. Barriers can be sorted into categories: e.g. external forces, other people, resources, and so on.

This 'wall' can then act as a trigger for discussion.

When the discussion is over, invite participants to break down the wall in whatever way they wish—as a symbol of breaking down the barriers they have identified.

Exercise 12.13: Seeing the Barrier

Group Structure: Individual visualisation followed by discussion.
Timing: 10 minutes.

Process: Ask participants to make themselves comfortable, close their eyes and breathe deeply to relax. Take them through the following visualisation:

Imagine yourself standing in front of a barrier. Notice the landscape you have created for yourself; is it bleak or lush?, hot or cold?, comfortable or harsh? Now notice the nature of the barrier: is it high or low?, thick or thin?, what is it made of? Let yourself experience how it feels to be standing in front of it. . . . Now imagine that you are able to get to the other side. . . . Notice how you accomplish this . . . and how it feels to have done it.

What is the landscape like now you are on the other side? . . . Turn round and look back at the barrier which held you up. How does it look now? . . . Turn back and imagine yourself moving forward.

Notes for the Trainer

What follows is a series of worksheets which are designed to help individuals clarify the nature of the work or lifestyle they would prefer as a starting point for their decision making and action plans. You can build a training session around them, giving people time to work through each one and coming together as a group to discuss the process. You could issue them at the end of a general training day for people to work on in their own time if they wish. Another possibility is to use a training session to design worksheets with the group. This is a useful and creative way to raise people's awareness of the range of matters to be thought through. In fact, the worksheets given here are the result of several such workshops.

My Ideal Picture 1

THE ENVIRONMENT

The idea behind this worksheet is to give you an opportunity to get a clear picture of the future job or life pattern for which you are hoping. The clearer your picture, the easier it will be to move towards it. Take your time to put this picture of yourself together.

Environment: Think about which kind of place would help you most in achieving what you want. Then consider the conditions of work under which you would be most satisfied.

Where: The place which would please me most and help me to achieve what I want out of work and life would be:

(List your most important needs: e.g. warm, near the sea, in a city centre, quiet, lively, easy access to art galleries, theatre, etc.)

1.
2.
3.
4.
5.
6.

Possible places would be:

1.
2.
3.

Conditions: I would be most happy and work most effectively if:

(List working conditions which are most important to you, e.g. most time spent indoors/outdoors, a lot of responsibility, own workspace, working alone/with others etc.)

1.
2.
3.
4.
5.

6.
7.
8.

When you have completed the lists, put them in order of priority. One way of doing this is to ask yourself: 'If I was offered two jobs, one of which was in an area which had factor 1 but not factor 2 and the other which had factor 2 but not factor 1, which would I choose?' Place a tick by which one you would choose and then go on to ask yourself this question about all the factors. At the end of the exercise the item with most ticks would be first on the list, the one with next most would be second and so on.

My Ideal Picture 2

VALUES

There is more to life than the physical setting in which you would prefer to work and live. We all have our own particular set of values. These may include beliefs about behaviour which is acceptable or unacceptable, personal responsibility, community, religion, morality, justice and so on. If we find ourselves in an environment where we are expected to put these values to one side, we are likely to end up feeling uncomfortable and unhappy. This worksheet is about the spiritual/emotional setting you would prefer.

The values which are important to me:

1.
2.
3.
4.
5.
6.
7.
8.

When you have completed your list, mark any items which are especially important. For instance, you may have reminded yourself that you want to be part of a team where people are supportive and helpful to you, or that you want to be trusted with responsibility.

My Ideal Picture 3a

IDENTIFYING SKILLS

The next step is to identify the skills which you take with you into your new job or new life phase. What follows is a list of skills. Give each one a number according to your assessment of your level of skill: 0 = I cannot (or do not want to) do this at all . . . 5 = I am very good at this. (Add any of your skills which are not in the lists)

Physical Skills

. . . . . Using my hands (e.g. sign language; massage)
. . . . . Finger dexterity (e.g. playing an instrument)
. . . . . Eye–hand co-ordination (e.g. games like tennis)
. . . . . Whole body physical co-ordination (e.g. aerobics)
. . . . . Agility, speed, strength or stamina

Skill with Materials, Objects, Machinery

. . . . . Craft (e.g. sewing, weaving, knitting, etc.)
. . . . . Cutting, carving, carpentry
. . . . . Painting, decorating, restoring
. . . . . Preparing, cooking food
. . . . . Precision work with tools
. . . . . Making, producing, manufacturing
. . . . . Maintaining, preserving, repairing
. . . . . Setting up or assembling machinery
. . . . . Operating, controlling or driving
. . . . . Planning, decorating
. . . . . Constructing, reconstructing
. . . . . Making videos, films, audio tapes

Skills with Living Things: Animals, Plants

. . . . . Gardening, cultivating flowers and vegetables
. . . . . Forestry
. . . . . Training animals
. . . . . Treating sick animals
. . . . . Raising animals

Skills with People (Individuals)

. . . . . Serving, helping, taking instructions
. . . . . Communicating face-to-face or on the phone
. . . . . Communication in writing
. . . . . Language skills
. . . . . Teaching, tutoring, training, instructing

. . . . . Advising, coaching, counselling, mentoring
. . . . . Supervising, managing
. . . . . Diagnosing, treating, healing
. . . . . Recruiting, motivating
. . . . . Selling
. . . . . Representing others
. . . . . Negotiating, resolving conflict
. . . . . Interviewing, selecting
. . . . . Working with children

Skills with People (Groups)
. . . . . Communicating effectively to a group
. . . . . Performing, entertaining, playing an instrument, singing
. . . . . Teaching, training, designing educational events
. . . . . Leading group discussions
. . . . . Running a business
. . . . . Managing a department

Skills with Ideas
. . . . . Compiling, searching, researching
. . . . . Inventing, designing new ideas
. . . . . Computing, working with numbers, accounting
. . . . . Analysing, organising information, classifying
. . . . . Visualising, drawing, painting
. . . . . Storing, filing
. . . . . Keeping records
. . . . . Information retrieval

My Ideal Picture 3b

SKILLS

In order to do the job I prefer well, I need the following skills:

1.
2.
3.
4.
5.
6.

> 7.
> 8.

My Ideal Picture 3c

CHARACTERISTICS

Here are some further questions to help you identify characteristics which will influence how happy and effective you will be; tick the answers which describe you best

My style of doing things is:
- [ ] slow and careful
- [ ] speedy—I like to work quickly
- [ ] calm
- [ ] thorough
- [ ] creative
- [ ] cautious
- [ ] dynamic

add your own items: . . .

When carrying out a task I:
- [ ] take the initiative
- [ ] prefer to handle a variety of tasks and responsibilities
- [ ] take risks
- [ ] get things done
- [ ] invite others to help

I like to:
- [ ] do things ahead of time
- [ ] find ways of speeding things up
- [ ] meet deadlines
- [ ] just get things done in time
- [ ] take my time however long it takes
- [ ] avoid meeting deadlines

In general, I:
- [ ] like my work space to be neat and orderly
- [ ] like attending to details
- [ ] am happy with repetitive routines
- [ ] like having responsibility for a complete process
- [ ] am excited by change
- [ ] work well under pressure

☐ like travelling
☐ prefer to work indoors/outdoors
☐ am good at responding to emergencies

My Ideal Picture 4

PEOPLE

This worksheet focuses on your people preferences. If you know you want to work with people, take some time now to think about which people you would most enjoy being with.

The kind of people I prefer to help/serve:
☐ Women
☐ Men
☐ Elderly people
☐ Middle-aged people
☐ Students
☐ Adolescents
☐ Children
☐ Infants
☐ Individuals
☐ Groups
☐ Couples
☐ People of a particular cultural background
☐ People of a particular social background
☐ People with a particular religious belief
☐ People who are ill
Add your own items: . . .

The problems I prefer to work with/solve:
☐ Physical difficulties
☐ Mental difficulties
☐ Career development
☐ Educational development
☐ Organisational training needs
☐ Relationship-based
☐ Personal development
☐ Behavioural change
Add your own items: . . .

When you have selected the area of problems which interest you most, note down any particular aspects to which you are particularly attracted (e.g. physical problems: overweight, disease, holistic treatments, addictions, etc.).

People I would prefer as colleagues:
- [ ] Women
- [ ] Men
- [ ] Young
- [ ] Middle-aged
- [ ] Elderly
- [ ] Any age
- [ ] Expert in their field
- [ ] Highly experienced
- [ ] Willing to learn
- [ ] Co-operative in their attitude and methods of work
- [ ] People of a particular cultural background
- [ ] People of a particular social background
- [ ] People of a particular religious background

Add your own items: . . .

My Ideal Picture 5a

INFORMATION WORK

If working with information is one of your preferences, use this worksheet to help you clarify your options.

Forms of Information:
- [ ] Books
- [ ] Magazines
- [ ] Newspapers
- [ ] Mail order catalogues
- [ ] Computer generated
- [ ] Visual
- [ ] Written
- [ ] Education text books
- [ ] Accounts
- [ ] Design blue-prints

Add your own items: . . .

My Ideal Picture 5b

USING THE INFORMATION

Think about the kind of uses to which you would want to put the information you produce or work with.

☐ Making recommendations/goal setting
☐ Drawing up action plans
☐ Finding solutions
☐ Making policy
☐ Designing systems
☐ Education
☐ Research

Add your own items: . . .

My Ideal Picture 6

OUTCOMES

This worksheet helps you to be clear about your objectives so that you can direct all your efforts towards the kind of outcome you want to achieve. Mark any of these categories that are important to you.

☐ *Possessions* . . . reputation/money/status/house/own business/ . . .
☐ *Authority* . . . to be in control of others/to make decisions/to be in charge/responsibility for organising/ . . .
☐ *Challenge* . . . competition/combat/ . . .
☐ *Success* . . . recognition/to be best/ . . .
☐ *Excitement* . . . risk/adventure/unpredictability/ . . .
☐ *Influence* . . . to affect people's lives/to make a difference/ . . .
☐ *Development* . . . of my own potential/others' potential/opportunity to learn new skills/ . . .
☐ *Contact* . . . to be part of a team/to work with people/ . . .
☐ *Security* . . . safety/predictability/to know you will be able to provide for your own and your family's needs/ . . .
☐ *Service* . . . to help others/to 'right wrongs'/ . . .
☐ *Enjoyment* . . . fun/stimulation/to feel happy/ . . .

Add your own items: . . .

Another approach to clarifying your wants and needs is to think in the long term about what you want to have achieved in your life as a whole. One way of doing this is to ask yourself what you want to have accomplished before you die. Make a list of everything that comes to mind—however impossible it seems. You never know when an opportunity might present itself to help you achieve something you want. The clearer you are about your long-term goals the more likely you are to recognise these chances when they come along.

My Ideal Picture 7

REMUNERATION

Money isn't the only reward to be gained from working, but it is important to most of us. Decide upon the minimum and maximum salary you would want. The minimum is the amount you need in order to provide basic requirements: food, rent, mortgage and so on. The maximum is the amount you would like to earn to enable you to do all the things you would like to do with your life. Write the amounts on the scale:

Minimum . . . . *Maximum*

Now think about what plans/decisions you should make to enable you to earn what you need. Do you need to:

☐ *increase your qualifications* (e.g. enrol for adult education courses of study/day release/evening classes/ . . .)?

☐ *develop your skill* (e.g. take up training opportunities within your organisation for skill development/enrol for courses of study outside organisation/consider opportunities for learning new skills in voluntary community work/ . . .)?

☐ *build up your confidence* (e.g. attend assertiveness training/learn relaxation techniques/reduce your stress/ . . .)?

☐ *change career direction* (e.g. look for different job/take management training/ . . .)?

☐ *become more flexible* (e.g. consider different ways of using your present experience and skill/consider part-time or sessional working/ . . .)?

☐ *become healthier* (e.g. stop smoking/take more exercise/consult doctor/ . . .)?

Add your own items: . . .

Notes for the Trainer

This ends the first chapter of Part IV which aims to help people to analyse their present situation and begin to consider the options open to them. The next chapter deals with how people can actually move towards their aims.

13

GETTING WHERE YOU WANT TO BE

The focus of the previous chapter was on clarifying as precisely as possible where people were at the present time in their working lives and what kind of changes they wanted to make. In this chapter the emphasis is on the next stage, which is to begin the practical measures which will make it possible for people to make the changes they want.

SESSION 27: CLOSING THE GAP

Training Objectives

1. To focus on planning and carrying out action for change.
2. To provide structure to identify and clarify intentions.
3. To consider alternative courses of action.
4. To plan first steps.

Trainer Input

In the last session we considered the process of, firstly, looking at where we are now in our working lives and, secondly, where we want to be. This session is about closing the gap. We are now going to move from understanding into planning and doing. Planning involves weighing up the situation. Doing this means

- prioritising and clarifying aims or intentions
- generating alternative courses of action
- evaluating the various courses open to you
- deciding which course of action to take.

    Taking action means

- the first stages of planning what you are going to do
- carrying out the first stage
- reviewing progress and moving on the next stage.

Before we do that, let us think about how you tend to take action.

Exercise 13.1: Taking Action

Group Structure: Individual questionnaire, which can be completed alone or discussed with a partner.
Timing: Up to 30 minutes.
Materials: Copy of questionnaire for each participant.

YOUR DECISION-MAKING STYLE QUESTIONNAIRE

1. Describe how you usually (a) choose between competing aims and goals and (b) decide on priorities. List the factors you tend to take into account. Are there any other factors which you ignore but which might be useful to consider?
2. Do you generate a range of options before you decide? If so, how do you decide between them?
3. Bring to mind two or three difficult decisions you have made recently. What were the difficulties? Were other people involved? What did you decide to do? How successful were you in meeting your aims? How were you left feeling about your actions? Is there anything you would do differently now?
4. In looking at the two or three situations you identified above, can you see any patterns in how you respond to decision making?
5. When things do not go well, how do you tend to respond?
6. If someone who knew you well were to answer these questions about you, would there be any differences in the answers?
7. Do you want to change anything in your way of approaching decision making as a result of thinking about these questions?

Trainer Input

We are all faced with many issues and questions about which we have to make choices, take action, decide on plans. With some of them it is easy to know where to start, so we just go ahead; at other times we need to stop to make sure we are taking the wisest action. The questions you have just answered may have illuminated the way you usually go about deciding what to do and, as a result, you might be thinking of taking a slightly more systematic approach.

The first step is to identify the issues which are or will be affected by any decision you make. For example:

- *Work*, including the expectations of you from others – managers and/or subordinates; achieving your objectives; maintaining good relationships; dealing with conflict; etc.
- *People*, including attitudes of others towards you; relationships which may be affected by your actions; unresolved conflicts; etc.
- *Your life*, including issues arising from your own particular history; recognising your strengths and weaknesses; ambitions; family matters; coming to terms with the ageing process; etc.
- *Yourself*, including your health; your personality; your style of work; etc.

All of these matters—even though they may seem to have no immediate relevance to the particular problem you are struggling with at the moment—can have a crucial influence on the success of your endeavours, so they are well worth thinking about.

This stage is rather like ensuring that you have an accurate map before starting out on a journey into new territory. Here is a technique to help you to begin to create your own map.

Exercise 13.2: Mapping the Territory

Group Structure: Individual work followed by discussion.
Timing: 30 minutes.

Process: This is a technique which can be used right through the decision-making and action process. It involves drawing a series of concentric circles with you at the centre—as if you were drawing a wheel. Then divide up the 'board' into sections, one for each matter which is an issue in your progress at the moment.

In the first segment, the one nearest you, write in each question or problem you are facing. In the next, write a brief description of how things are and what you have already done with regard to each particular item. The next circle is for you to enter how you would like things to be, i.e. what it is you are aiming for. The circle after that is for all the possible courses of action that could lead you to your aim, and the final circle is for the first steps you intend to take, (Figure 13.1).

Give participants large sheets of paper on which they can draw their 'decision wheel'.

This exercise is a good way of clarifying the things you must do to achieve the

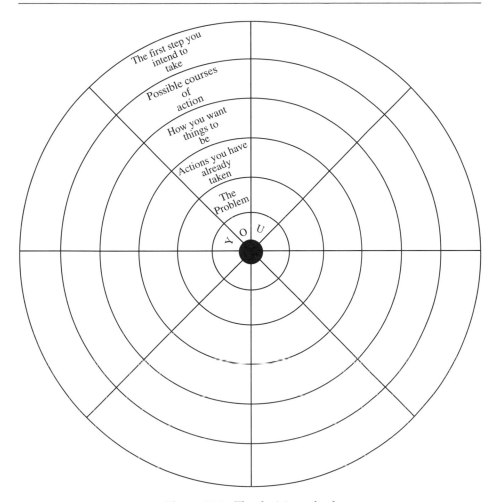

Figure 13.1: The decision wheel

end result you want. Probably the most difficult ring to complete is the one in which you decide on your first step: your priority for action. There are various questions which you could ask yourself as an aid to your decision:

- Is there some aspect which is the most important/which matters most/ which will have the greatest advantage to you or others?
- Is there some aspect which will show results more quickly than others?
- Do time limits affect any aspects of the situation so that if you don't take action your options will be limited?
- Is there an aspect which could be said to be more urgent than others?
- Is there some aspect which would be easier than any other to begin with?
- Is there one aspect which is linked to many others so affecting a wide range of problems if it is resolved?

- Is there one aspect which, for you, would be the greatest challenge—and most rewarding—to achieve?

Exercise 13.3: Priority for First Steps

Group Structure: Pairs.
Timing: 15 minutes.

Process: Ask participants to refer to their own map and, in pairs, to ask each other the questions listed above with the aim of deciding on their first steps.

Having deciding on the first steps you could take, let us consider how to give yourself as many options as possible. The reason for this is that if you only have one action plan which, for one reason or another, does not succeed, you have to start from the beginning again—or be tempted to give the whole thing up. On the other hand, if you have several courses of action, you can just move on to your second choice. You can work at two levels at this stage. For some of your first steps it will be relatively simple to generate different options by using a technique such as the brainstorming described in Chapter 8 (see page 133). For instance, to improve your general health you might have decided to take more exercise. You could start attending your local gym, take a brisk walk twice a day, swim regularly, join an aerobics class, and so on. However, things are not always so obvious as this and you may have to work at a deeper level to decide on your strategies. Mike Pedlar and Tom Boydell (1985) suggest that you basically have four general strategies when facing difficult situations. You can take any of the following actions.

- *Decide to change things*—e.g. face someone with whom you are in conflict, ask for a salary increase, improve the system which has caused a problem, take on more staff, etc.
- *Decide to change yourself*—e.g. become more assertive, improve your health, think about how changing your behaviour might change the situation, learn a new skill, etc.
- *Decide to leave things well alone*—e.g. deciding NOT to take action can often be a wise decision. You may, for instance, realise that making the change you want will hurt or create problems for others. It may be that living with the situation may not be as bad as you think, particularly if you realise that if you do make this decision it would be a waste of time and energy to continue grumbling about it.
- *Decide to leave the situation altogether*—e.g. to move house, look for a new job, etc.

It is obvious how whichever of these strategies you decide upon will affect the action you take.

Exercise 13.4: Alternative Courses of Action

Group Structure: Pairs.
Timing: 30 minutes.

Process: Ask participants, working in pairs, to take one of the items from their map and work with each other discussing the implications of each strategic approach described above. Ask them to rate the four strategies in terms of preference.

Notes for the Trainer

The exercises and explanations you provide depend on the experience and previous training of the group. For instance, a technique like force field analysis would be useful to introduce here. If the group are already familiar with the process you could suggest they continued working on the examples they have taken from their own 'map'. If they are not, explain the process, perhaps providing a case study for practice. Here is a structure for introducing the concept.

Trainer Input

Force field analysis is a way of improving your chances of actually achieving what you are setting out to do. It is a method of examining what is involved in the changes we may be thinking about making, identifying which forces might be helpful and which might hinder progress.

Exercise 13.5: Force Field Analysis

Group Structure: Trainer input followed by practice.
Timing: 30 minutes.
Materials: Flip chart.

Process: Having explained to the group how force field analysis might help them, draw a horizontal line in the centre of the flip chart. Explain that this represents the present situation; now at the left-hand side draw a vertical line, with an arrow pointing upwards, representing the intention. Now ask the group to brainstorm anything they feel will affect the situation. If, for instance, you have chosen 'Taking more exercise' as your example, they might offer:

Cost of membership expensive; companionship of other people; feeling of achievement as health improves; feeling more in control; difficulty of finding time; it would be fun; take some time for effects to show; would become stronger physically and so on.

Each of these can be shown as either helping or hindering continuing success and can be drawn above or below the line, as shown in Figure 13.2.

Now suggest that participants work on their own or on a case study example. As each item is analysed in this way, the action with most positive potential often becomes clear.

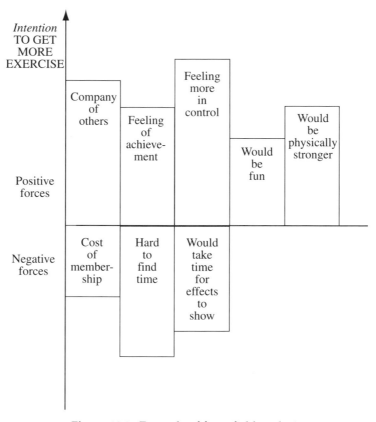

Figure 13.2: Example of force field analysis

Another approach, if you have generated several options, is to consider each one in terms of losses or costs and gains or benefits. Let us look at an example.

Exercise 13.6: Losses and Gains

Group Structure: Trainer input followed by personal work and discussion.
Timing: 30 minutes.
Materials: Flip chart for trainer demonstration.

Process: Decide on the example you wish to use—for instance, you might take someone who is deciding on their future progress. Their options are to:

- stay in the present job and wait for promotion
- look at a more senior position in the present department
- look elsewhere in the company for a more senior position
- seek for a transfer in the present company to a different area of work, thus changing career direction
- look outside the present company for a more senior position in the same line of work
- look outside the present company for a different line of work.

Write the first option at the top of the flip chart. Divide the page vertically down the middle and head the left-hand column *Costs* and the right-hand column *Benefits*. Inviting the group to make their suggestions, listing the various possible advantages and disadvantages. The list might look like:

STAYING AND WAITING FOR PROMOTION

Costs	*Benefits*
Promotion might never come.	The job is familiar and I feel confident in doing it.
No change of scene or people.	I will not lose contact with the people I like
Lack of challenge.	Lack of stress.
I will feel stuck.	I need not worry about moving house or children's schools, etc.
I may have to compete with others in the company	

When the list is finished, the next stage is to give each item a rating so that you can begin to develop a picture of just how much the advantages and disadvantages should influence your decision.

You can continue the exercise by asking the group to repeat this process for each option and place the 'balance sheets' next to each other and examine them. Give them time to think about or talk through their observations. They are looking for any options which seem on balance to give most of what is wanted without too great a cost.

We have spent some time exploring how you might achieve your aims so that there is nothing left to do but get on with it! Thinking and talking is very useful, but in themselves they do not achieve change—things only change when you do something. So now you need an action plan. Let us summarise where we are so far and set out the steps for an action plan, then you will have a chance to make a plan for yourself.

1. Clearly define your objectives; too many plans fail because the desired result is not stated clearly enough.
2. Start with your first steps: i.e. what you are going to do now. If you move ahead too quickly you will probably trip over yourself. Think of a baby learning to walk: if he or she tried to run first, what is likely to happen?
3. When you decide on your various action steps, be very specific. Another reason action plans fail is because they are stated too generally to be useful. 'I'll speak up more at meetings' is not as good as 'At next week's meeting I will speak at least twice'.
4. Make sure the steps are in a logical order. If you are, for instance, planning to speak to your boss about something you will first probably have to make an appointment.
5. Write a review date into your action plan so that you can make modifications if necessary.

Exercise 13.7: Making an Action Plan

Group Structure: Individual work.
Timing: 30 minutes
Materials: An Action Planning Sheet, a blank sheet of writing paper and an envelope for each participant.

Process: Hand out the planning sheets and give participants time to complete it.

Next, ask all participants to write themselves a letter, describing what they want to have achieved in six months, how they feel about the action plan they have devised, and giving themselves the kind of en- couragement that they feel would most motivate them. Ask them to sign the letter and put it in the envelope, which they should then address to themselves. The envelopes can then be collected by you. Alternatively, each person can give his or her envelope to a member of the group and take that person's envelope. In either approach, the envelope should be posted in six months' time!

ACTION PLANNING WORKSHEET
Develop an action plan for each of your objectives in turn.

My first objective is . . . .

. . . .

The action steps I will take are (at this stage don't worry about putting them in sequence):

1.
2.
3.
4.

Now rewrite the list, putting them in the logical order for action:

1.
2.
3.
4.

I will start with the first step on (date): . . . .

I will review progress on (date): . . . .

I expect to reach the objectives by (date): . . . .

Notes for the Trainer

This is the last session in this component of the course. There may be opportunities for you to provide support for individuals through review sessions or follow-up training days. The actual process of putting action plans into play can be difficult, and constructive support can make the difference between success and failure. If you, as the trainer, will have no further contact with the group you might consider adding the following sessions to your course.

SESSION 28: WHAT IF THINGS DON'T WORK OUT?

Training Objectives

1. To explore how to create a support structure.
2. To counter self-defeating beliefs.
3. To create a self-care stress-reducing programme.

Trainer Input

Even though we have been very careful about sticking to the guidelines in deciding our action plan, we cannot control everything. There will always be outside factors that can result in lack of success and, because we are human, we will probably make some mistakes—or we might even change our mind as we begin to experience the effects of change.

Whatever the reason, this means that we will sometimes have to face up to disappointment and it is always a good thing to be prepared for this eventuality. It is realistic to be aware of the possibility that some of our plans may not work out and have a method of coping if this should occur.

Exercise 13.8: What Happens if you are Disappointed?

Group Structure: Personal exercise followed by discussion.
Timing: 15 minutes.

Process: Ask participants to think back to a particular disappointment in their life and jot down brief details.

Ask them to recall their first reactions: thoughts, feelings, behaviour. Ask if these are typical reactions, then ask participants to write down how they usually face up to disappointments now.

There are certain things which usually help us face situations like these. For instance, finding a way of discharging the bad feelings we usually experience is important. If we were to look at the list of feelings you remembered just now, we would probably notice quite a range. We can feel angry, frightened, helpless, hopeless, resentful, depressed, anxious. Getting rid of these feelings is important because they can remain within us and contribute to the build-up of stress, making it much more difficult for us to proceed. How you do this is very much a personal matter: crying, shouting, beating a cushion, digging the garden, a hard game of squash, a long walk—anything which will physically enable you to let the feeling out. This in itself will not solve the particular problem—but you will feel some relief and be more able to face up to things.

Going back to the exercise you have just completed, can you see whether you are effectively discharging negative feelings and, if not, do you have ideas as to how you can begin?

Another good way of getting over difficult times is to know you have someone to talk to. One problem many of us have given ourselves is to expect most of our emotional support to come from one or two people. Probably an intimate partner, a spouse, parent, close friend—but if you stop and think about it for a moment you would see that it doesn't really make a lot of sense to expect one or two people to be able to meet all our needs. The next exercise is to help you identify who is in your support network and whether there are any gaps which you might need to fill.

Exercise 13.9: Who to Talk To?

Group Structure: Individual work.
Timing: 20 minutes.
Materials: Support Network Worksheet for each participant.

Process: Hand out the worksheets, explaining that at different times we all need different kinds of support. The idea behind the worksheet is for participants to write in the names of people who fulfil their various needs.

PERSONAL SUPPORT NETWORK WORKSHEET
Write in the names of people you know who provide you with these different kinds of support.

Types of support	*Person's name*
Someone I can always rely on	. . . .
Someone I enjoy chatting to	. . . .
Someone who I can rely on to make me feel valued and competent	. . . .
Someone who I can trust to give me honest and constructive feedback	. . . .
Someone who is knowledgeable about the matters I might need help with	. . . .
Someone who isn't afraid to challenge me to look at things differently	. . . .
Someone who I can depend on in a crisis	. . . .

Someone who makes me laugh   . . . .

Someone with whom I can share my feelings   . . . .

Someone with whom I can share personal
good and bad news   . . . .

Someone who gives me new ideas   . . . .

Add any needs of your own which are not
listed:

Someone who   . . . .

Someone who   . . . .

There are a number of questions you need to ask when you have
completed this list:

- Is there anything that surprises you?
- Are there any gaps?
- Are you relying on one or two people for your support; if so, does this matter? What might the consequences be for you and for them?
- Is there any way in which you want to modify your existing support network?

Another element in getting through disappointing times is the capacity many of us have to create impossible expectations of ourselves through the belief systems we develop. Here is what tends to happen when something does not go right. Firstly, we experience the happening (or non-happening); then we tell ourselves something about it; then we have a feeling about what we have told ourselves; and then we take action on the basis of that feeling.

Take Jonathon, for example, who has just failed a job interview. He receives the letter telling him that he has not been offered the job; so he tells himself 'I'm pathetic; I should have been able to do better. I'll never be good enough. I'm not going to put myself though that again—I'll never apply for another job.' So he ends up feeling ashamed, frustrated, hopeless. In response to these feelings he might well decide not to continue in his search for a new job.

Remember:

- What you think affects how you feel and what you do.
- You can probably take more control over your thoughts than you assume you can.
- Controlling how you think puts you much more in control of yourself.

For any of you who are doubtful about whether you can actually control how you think, see the next exercise.

Exercise 13.10: Pink Elephants?

Timing: 5 minutes

Process: Tell the group that this is an experiment in thought control, and ask them to sit comfortably and close their eyes. Tell them to conjure up in their mind the image of a pink elephant and give them time to do this—it will take some people longer than others. Ask them to indicate they have this image by raising their hand. When everyone has completed this part of the exercise, tell them to change the image they have into that of a green parrot! Once again give people time to do this, encouraging people to stick with it until they have succeeded. Eventually, everyone does.

This simple exercise demonstrates that it is possible to control one's thoughts. Changing pink elephants into green parrots is not going to control those external events or pressures that are affecting you—but changing how you are thinking can, in turn, affect how you feel and react to what's happening.

Barrie Hopson and Mike Scally (1984) compiled a list of beliefs which they label as self-defeating:

1. I must be loved or liked by everyone, people should love me.
2. I must be perfect in all I do.
3. All the people with whom I work or live must be perfect.
4. I can have little control over what happens to me.
5. It is easier to avoid facing difficulties than to deal with them.
6. Disagreement and conflict are a disaster and must be avoided at all costs.
7. People, including me, do not change.
8. Some people are always good; others always bad.
9. The world should be perfect and it is terrible and unbearable that it is not.
10. People are fragile and need to be protected from 'The Truth'.
11. Other people exist to make us happy and we cannot be happy unless they do so.
12. Crises are invariable and entirely destructive and no good can come from them.
13. Somewhere there is the perfect job, the perfect 'solution', the perfect partner, etc., and all we need to do is search for them.
14. We should not have problems. If we do it means we are incompetent.
15. There is only one way of seeing any situation, i.e. the 'True way'.

Think about the last time you felt bad about something. Can you remember what you were telling yourself at the time? Do you think that any of these beliefs influenced your reaction? The following exercise may show you how important your thoughts are.

Exercise 13.11: Self-defeating Beliefs

Group Structure: Individual work followed by discussion.
Timing: 20 minutes.
Materials: Self-defeating Belief Worksheet for each participant.

Process: Give people time to complete the worksheet.

SELF-DEFEATING BELIEFS WORKSHEET (1)

Complete the sheet by writing down what you tell yourself in your own words—don't hold back. No one but you will see this worksheet, and the more honest you are the more chance you have of identifying the belief system that may be hindering your progress. You may, for instance, be full of condemnation of yourself, others or the world in general; or become very patronising, sure of what everyone else should be doing; or experience very depressing thoughts of hopelessness. Whatever they are, write them down. You need to start by thinking of a recent event which ended up unsatisfactorily for you so that you ended up feeling bad.

The Event:

What I told myself during and after the event:

What I felt:

What I did:

The belief(s) on which I was acting:

When participants have completed their worksheets, invite people to mention any of the beliefs from the list which they may have identified as playing some part in their thinking. It is useful to take each belief in turn and consider how acting on it can influence one's actions. When the discussion has run its course, give out the second worksheet:

SELF-DEFEATING BELIEFS WORKSHEET (2)

It is time now to challenge your belief system. For instance, you know that it is not possible to love and be loved by everyone. So telling yourself that this is not only possible, but that you are failing unless it is true, is clearly counter-productive. You need to change the absolutes into choices.

Change each of the following statements into one which allow you a choice. The first statement has been completed as an example.

1. I must be loved or liked by everyone, people should love me
could become:

1. *In the same way that I choose who I love or like, so will other people. I can't expect everyone to love or like me. The important thing is that I can respect myself.*

2. I must be perfect in all I do.

3. All the people with whom I work or live must be perfect.

4. I can have little control over what happens to me.

5. It is easier to avoid facing difficulties than to deal with them.

6. Disagreement and conflict are a disaster and must be avoided at all costs.

7. People, including me, do not change.

8. Some people are always good; others always bad.

9. The world should be perfect and it is terrible and unbearable that it is not.

10. People are fragile and need to be protected from 'The Truth'.

11. Other people exist to make us happy and we cannot be happy unless they do so.

12. Crises are invariable and entirely destructive and no good can come from them.

13. Somewhere there is the perfect job, the perfect 'solution', the perfect partner, etc., and all we need to do is search for them.

14. We should not have problems. If we do it means we are incompetent.

15. There is only one way of seeing any situation, i.e. the 'True way'.

Notes for the Trainer

When people put efforts into making changes and do not succeed as much or as quickly as they want, they are bound to feel disappointed. This disappointment can lead to feeling very stressed. You might introduce at this point in the session some of the stress-reducing strategies described in Chapter 9.

If you haven't time to include these exercises, you can end the session with some reference to the idea.

Trainer Input

There are various ways of dissipating stress. For instance, developing a regular fitness programme which might include exercise, dancing, brisk walking, aerobics, football, jogging or whatever takes your fancy. Stress can make us feel very tired, and stimulating activity is a good way of getting to feel better and increase your energy.

Looking after your mind is as important as re-energising your body, so listening to music, reading, meditating, spending time with people you like, going to a film or a play can all help to decrease your stress level.

You can also work directly on your body by massage, deep breathing, yoga, Tai-Chi and so on.

There is no blueprint for a self-care stress-reduction programme—each of us can create our own so that we are able to look after ourselves when the going is rough.

REFERENCES

Hopson, B. & Scally, M. (1984) *Build Your Own Rainbow*. Lifeskills Associates.
Pedlar, M. & Boydell, T. (1985) *Managing Yourself*. Fontana.

$\boxed{\textbf{14}}$

ENDINGS

So far the work in this part of the book has been appropriate for any staff groups wanting or needing to change or develop their career path for any reason. This last chapter focuses on those people for whom the next step will be ending their present employment because of either redundancy or retirement. The sessions already described in this part of the book can certainly be used to meet the needs of this group, encouraging them to consider their options and to think clearly about how they will manage the next stage of their life. However, this group may also have special needs. It is certainly true that both redundancy and retirement can trigger positive changes but they can also generate strong feelings: fear about the future, anger about lack of choice and so on. Trainers can help by providing practical information such as career opportunities, welfare rights, etc. They can also give people an opportunity to talk about their fears and worries, often a necessary and therapeutic prelude to the clarity of decision making which is needed at times like these.

It is not uncommon in the present job scene for a group, department or a whole organisation to close. In some cases, training is offered to those affected to help prepare them for their job search. Such courses might include interview skills, information inputs on rights and benefits and career advice. The following session could be incorporated, offering a personal focus and the opportunity for each person to think and talk about managing the situation in which they find themselves.

SESSION 29: SURVIVING REDUNDANCY

Training Objectives

1. To provide opportunity to express feelings.
2. To emphasise the importance of a positive attitude to job-hunting.
3. To prepare 'job-hunt personal charter'.

Trainer Input

The purpose of this session is to create the frame of mind which will help you most in making the next step in your working life. Our first task is to try to modify any negativity which may be a barrier to your moving as quickly and successfully as you want. There are different ways of viewing the present situation: for some of you it will be the push you know you needed to move on; for others a shockingly unexpected and unwanted situation. Some of you may be excited; others fearful; others angry. Our thoughts and feelings have great influence over what action we take and how we take it. Let us take a look at what's happening for you now.

Exercise 14.1: Unwanted Luggage

Group Structure: Individual work followed by general discussion.
Timing: 20 minutes.
Materials: Small notepad and one large sheet of paper and coloured pens for each person.

Process: Firstly, encourage participants to sit quietly and gather their thoughts about the situation. Suggest they close their eyes and let thoughts come and go, rather than focus on anything particular. No thought or feeling is unacceptable! The exercise works best when people allow themselves to be inhibited, acknowledging positive and negative reactions. Each time they are aware of a particular thought or feeling, ask them to jot down a word or symbol to represent it in their notepad. At the end of two or three minutes each person will have his or her own list.

The next part of the exercise is to draw a number of squares on the large sheet of paper. Each square represents a box (or suitcase). Tell participants to consider each of the thoughts and feelings they have identified. The idea is that they will keep those which they feel will be useful to them—i.e. thoughts and feelings which motivate, reassure or nurture—and box up those which will not be so useful—for instance, thoughts of revenge, hopelessness and so on. They should label each box with either the word or the symbol.

When this part of the exercise is finished, a general discussion can follow. When this has run its course, ask participants to think about how they want to deal with the drawing of their 'luggage'; they can choose an action to symbolise their intention, e.g. throw the whole paper away, tear

---

up some 'boxes' and keep others, carefully fold the paper up and put it somewhere safe. . . .

Notes for the Trainer

Obviously an exercise such as this does not aim to actually solve any of the problems people may be facing, but it can help to clarify how problems can be made worse by our own particular reactions—and how these reactions can be modified. It is important not to present the activity as a glib exercise in the 'positive-thinking-cure-all' mode but rather as one creative way of preparing for the work that is to come. Another way of opening up the emotional impact of redundancy is to approach the issue of loss. Being made redundant, downsized, reorganised, restructured, 'let go' or however the process was described, involves some profound losses to be faced.

Exercise 14.2: Dealing with Job Loss

Group Structure: Individual work and small group discussion.
Timing: 15 minutes.
Materials: Self-Assessment Worksheet for each participant.

Process: Hand out the worksheet and suggest that people mark any item with which they identify, explaining that they are all very natural reactions. A general discussion can follow —small groups might enable people to share some of their experiences. It is always comforting to realise you are not alone in your experience.

ON HEARING THE NEWS

Since hearing the news of redundancy, have you experienced any of these feelings?

anger	guilt
powerlessness	hopelessness
fear	anxiety
loss of self-esteem	loss of status
self-pity	wanting revenge
tiredness	impatience
confusion	physical illness
short temper	wanting to withdraw
not wanting to get up	sleeplessness
worry	loneliness

> Any other unusual reactions you have noticed:

Trainer Input

Just what do we lose when we lose a job?

Sense of Identity
The work we do is one important element in defining our sense of who we are. To lose it threatens our security; skills and knowledge in which we were confident suddenly feel less safe. Self-esteem can plummet as we wonder whether we are going to be good enough to get another job.

Pride
Most of us want to be proud of what we achieve and many of our achievements are tied up with work. It is difficult to maintain our sense of dignity and pride when our job is taken away. We can even feel shame or embarrassment, even though people are sympathetic about our plight. In some indefinable way, it all feels like our fault.

Personal Satisfaction
A lot of satisfaction comes from the feeling of a job well done; we know we're needed and we feel useful.

Financial Security
We do not only lose emotional security; money is what allows us to maintain our lifestyle. We still have to pay the bills and provide for our families. Being deprived of the means inevitably leads to worry.

   Handling these losses is not easy, although there are things that will help. For instance:

Getting Support
Our natural reaction to loss make it difficult to ask for or accept help which is offered. Realising that feeling embarrassed and shamed is irrational does not always stop the feelings—so our reaction may be to want to hide away. However, there are often good support networks in the community: churches, community groups, voluntary organisations, local authorities often initiate opportunities for both practical and emotional support.

Being Open to Change
Because of our human need for safety and security, we tend to be anxious when faced with change. However, this is a time for you to consider changing

the direction of your working life. Considering something does not commit you to anything, but if you are able to give yourself more options you are bound to feel (and actually are) more likely to succeed in your next step.

Share your Thoughts and Feelings

As we have seen, redundancy invariably produces emotions which are often hard to handle—especially alone. If you try to keep your reactions hidden they will find a way of expressing themselves—often to those who are closest to you. Discord in the family and the breakdown of close relationships can occur as a result of these communication problems.

Exercise 14.3: How to Deal with Loss

Group Structure: Small workshop groups.
Timing: 10 minutes.
Materials: Large sheets of paper and marker pen for each group.

Process: The point of this exercise is to give people some practical ways of dealing with the effects of loss. Each sheet of paper could have the following heading already printed:

A healthy plan for facing loss would include:

Invite participants to build up a list which could make up a set of guidelines for healthy grieving. The list could include:

Accept the sense of loss.	Express feelings openly to appropriate people.
Don't take action too quickly.	Take time to think.
Take care of physical health.	Have some fun.
Give each day a structure.	. . . and so on.

The world of work, like every other element of society, is constantly changing. Taking a look at history shows this. We could go back as far as the Stone Age. As far as we know 'work' for those communities was hunting, gathering, building homes and having babies. Life and work were not separate—the issue was survival. However, a big change came about as agriculture began to develop in places in which the climate was conducive to the planting of crops and the domestication of livestock. People became 'farmers' and built permanent homes. Working the land required tools, and so toolmakers and metalworkers came into being. Something very much like an economy began to exist as crop surpluses could be stored and traded. To move quickly through several centuries and come nearer our time, the world of work consisted of agriculture in the countryside and craftsmen and their apprentices in the towns. The Industrial Revolution—usually dated from 1769 when James Watt patented the first steam engine—led to enormous changes. For instance, in England in the year 1200 AD about 90% of the population lived on the land. By the beginning of the twentieth century these figures were more or less reversed, and now less than 3% of the population lives on the land (David Statt, 1994). These are just historical statistics, but of course every statistic like this covers a host of personal stories very much like our own: people having to adapt to changes they could not have foreseen; being uprooted from their homes with their skills no longer needed or valued. Society's wealth was based in industry—factories, mills, steel works and so on—and the ever-increasing production of goods required a transport and storage system—railways, steamships, warehouses, etc. And, of course, the process of change did not stop. Developing knowledge of physics, chemistry, biology brought about a 'light industry revolution'. If you were a blacksmith one hundred years ago you could look forward to steady and continuing employment. How could you have foreseen that Henry Ford's horseless carriage would one day take over from the horse? Types of work such as farming or mining rise, fall and almost disappear as, of course, do particular occupations. How many blacksmiths do you know? Companies, too, come and go. If you look at things in this way, change is inevitable. The 1990s are years of very profound change—probably the greatest of which is the way things have speeded up. In past generations, a son would almost be certain that he would be following in his father's footsteps (a daughter would probably know that her future did not include independent work!); it was possible to choose a career path and predict how this would develop over a life-time. This is not really the case for most people now. Workers from all different groups (white and blue collar, managerial, professional) are all subject to downsizing, restructuring, reorganisation—terms with which we are becoming increasingly familiar.

It's easy to become depressed if you fall victim to these upheavals in the working world. So to help keep a sense of balance, let us consider certain facts:

- Employment opportunities continue to exist. Even in the present climate, people still get promoted, move to other areas, change jobs, retire, get ill, get sacked—all events which create a job vacancy. So although it's easy to get into a hopeless frame of mind thinking there just are no jobs out there, it's important to remember that in fact there are vacancies.
- It is nearly always possible to reduce the cost of your lifestyle without

having to deprive yourself of everything that makes life worth living. Obviously, money is a major worry and careful budgeting is going to be necessary. If you have a redundancy financial package you will want to make the best possible use of it and, of course, you will want to get advice and information on benefits.

Let us now think about ways of reducing costs.

Exercise 14.4: Low-Cost Lifestyle Brainstorm

Group Structure: Brainstorm followed by discussion.
Timing: 15 minutes.

Process: Ask people to offer ideas for a low (or no) cost lifestyle; as in any brainstorm, encourage way out, eccentric ideas as well as 'sensible' suggestions. Here are some examples:

- Ask friends and neighbours for seeds and cuttings.
- Develop an interest in DIY.
- Start attending auctions, car boot sales, etc.
- Use diesel (cheaper than petrol) in car.
- Buy fresh food from markets rather than ready made.
- Make your own wine, jam, beer, preserves, etc.
- Instead of a holiday, plan a series of country walks, visit museums, art galleries, etc.
- Browse in book shops.
- Get home videos instead of going to cinema.

Being in a situation like this does make us redefine material values; things which seemed absolutely necessary to our happiness sometimes turn out not to be so important. We can find pleasure and practical benefits from other things which we may never have considered before.

Notes for the Trainer

This session will end with an opportunity for participants to write out their future action plan. You may choose to include sessions on decision making and objective setting (see page 195) and other sessions described earlier in the book which you feel may be useful at this point.

The next session in this chapter looks at endings from the point of view of retirement which, although not coming as such a shock as redundancy usually does, can also carry a powerful emotional charge and practical problems.

SESSION 30: PREPARING FOR RETIREMENT

Training Objectives

1. To explore feelings about retirement.
2. To brainstorm options.
3. To create plan for keeping healthy.

Notes for the Trainer

Pre-retirement courses can be a useful opportunity for people to clarify their ideas and create a plan for a happy retirement. As in the session on redundancy, as a trainer no doubt you will plan to present information about pensions and welfare benefits, local leisure facilities, post-retirement paid employment opportunities, voluntary work options and so on. This session can be included in such a course; its intention is to address the emotional impact of impending retirement and to consider the range of options available.

Trainer Input

Retirement is not what it used to be! At one time, retiring from a job was like retiring from active life. Sitting by the fire with slippers and pipe, contemplating the past, was probably the lifestyle which beckoned—perhaps enlivened by visits from the grandchildren. Now, however, for many people retirement is the start of an active, enjoyable and exciting phase and this session is the chance to begin to plan.

Retirement is usually thrust upon us whether or not we are ready for it. A self-employed person does have more choice, but most people choose to reduce their work commitments or retire completely. Being newly retired means facing gains and losses.

Exercise 14.5: Gains and Losses in Retirement

Group Structure: Brainstorm.
Timing: 5 minutes (longer if discussion ensues).

Process: Draw a line down the centre of a blank flip chart and write *Gains* on one side and *Losses* on the other. Then write in people's suggestions as they call them out. Gains might include more time for family, opportunity to travel, less stress; losses might include less (or no) contact with colleagues, reduced status, loneliness, fall in income and so on.

This short exercise might trigger an important discussion allowing participants to share their feelings—positive and negative—about their position.

There are several ingredients to a good retirement; one is that most people need to continue feeling useful to someone else. Another is retaining some sort of personal discipline and structure to the day—for instance, getting up at a reasonable time, eating proper meals, regular activities and so on. Another crucial element is maintaining good health.

Exercise 14.6: Hopes, Fears and Expectations

Group Structure: Small groups.
Timing: 20 minutes.

Process: Brief each group to compile lists of their hopes, fears and expectations with regard to retirement. These lists can be presented to the group as a whole, or someone from the small group can report on the discussion when the groups come together.

Each item can be discussed so that participants have a chance to know that they are not alone in their feelings. When discussing the fears it is usually possible to find a way of reducing or even dismissing them altogether.

Having analysed concerns and hopes it is logical to identify any blocks which may hinder your successful transition to retirement.

Exercise 14.7: Blocks to Transition

Group Structure: Group discussion.
Timing: 20 minutes.

Process: The discussion should focus around blocks which participants believe might stand in the way of successfully making the transition to retirement. As blocks are identified, they should be recorded on a flip chart. This list will act as the trigger for the next exercise.

Our next task is to decide on the strategies which would allow us to move forward in the way we want.

Exercise 14.8: Moving on Graffiti

Group Structure: Individual followed by discussion.
Timing: 30–45 minutes.
Materials: The lists of blocks drawn up in the previous exercise; large sheets of wall chart paper and coloured pens for each participant.

Process: Take each block (or category of blocks) and, using one blank wall chart sheet of paper for each, write it as a heading. Then display the sheets of paper around the room. Invite everyone to walk around the room and write any ideas they have for getting through the blocks on the appropriate sheet of paper. When they have finished, give them time to read each sheet and consider the ideas.

This exercise leads to the next in which people can start their life plan for the future. It should include short- and long-term plans, budgeting details, decisions about continuing work if desired, leisure activities, health care plan and so on. It is a very personal exercise so it would depend on the nature of the group as to whether you decide to hold a discussion. You may have the opportunity to offer personal consultations for any participant who would like to discuss his or her plan.

As we near the end of this session, there is one more exercise to set you on your path.

Exercise 14.9: Road to the Future Visualisation

Timing: 10 minutes.

Process: After inviting people to make themselves comfortable, close their eyes and breathe deeply, take them through this final visualisation:

Imagine you are walking along a path. You have been on a long journey and you know that this path will take you towards your destination. Take time to notice the nature of the terrain you are walking through. However hard the journey has been, you are now moving into easier territory. Allow yourself to do this and to enjoy the change. . . . As you turn the next corner you see a hill ahead of you. You continue to move ahead climbing the gentle slope. . . . When you reach the top, you see a seat and sit down. You are looking out over a vista which you can create in your mind. The scene on which you are looking down is inviting, and when you are ready you will descend the hill to become part of it. . . . It represents your future and though in a moment we will return to the present and to this room, you can visit the scene whenever you like. . . . Use it to help you make the decisions about creating the future you want for yourself.

REFERENCE

Statt, D. (1994). *Psychology and the World of Work.* Macmillan Press.

INDEX

Index compiled by Liza Weinkove

Related titles of interest...

International Handbook of Selection and Assessment
Edited by Neil Anderson and Peter Herriot

"... reads like the 'who's who' of cutting-edge thinking... this book is a fantastic resource!"

Talya N. Bauer, Ph.D., Portland State University, UKSA
0-471-96638-X   680pp   1997   Hardback

Personnel Selection
Third Edition: Adding Value Through People
Mark Cook

Deals with psychological processes and methods for the assessment of personnel abilities and qualities and also with the social and organisational issues related to selection.

0-471-98156 7   368pp   1998   Hardback
0-471-98158-3   368pp   1998   Paperback

Handbook of Work and Health Psychology
Edited by Marc J. Schabracq, Jacques A.M. Winnubst and Cary L. Cooper

Describes the field and surveys illness and health in different occupations and in different parts of the world.

0-471-95789-5   512pp   1996   Hardback

Handbook of Work Group Psychology
Edited by Michael West

Provides a comprehensive, critical and up-to-date overview of all the key areas of group psychology in the context of organisational and work groups.

0-471-95790-9   642pp   1996   Hardback

Visit the Wiley Home Page at http:\\www.wiley.co.uk